GET OVER YOURSELF

A juicy and refreshing reminder of the
things that matter in life.

GET OVER YOURSELF

A juicy and refreshing reminder of the things that matter in life.

Jack Horton

This book is dedicated to everyone who has made a profound impact on my life - **you know who you are**

Table Of Contents

Introduction
Intro... 1

Chapter 1
Enjoy The Moment 7

Chapter 2
Say Fuck It Regularly 23

Chapter 3
Be Glass Half Full 33

Chapter 4
Be Unsocial 49

Chapter 5
Be Differently United 67

Chapter 6
Get Out Of The Comfort Zone 79

Chapter 7
Control The Comparison 95

Chapter 8
Don't Hate Appreciate 115

Chapter 9
Be Kind 133

Chapter 10
Don't Drop You Moral Compass 147

Conclusion
The End Is Nigh 163

Thank You's
I Count My Blessings 171

*"I have no special talent. I
am only passionately curious."*

Albert Einstein

INTRODUCTION

INTRO...

L adies and gents, boys and girls, and all you beautiful folks floating somewhere in between - gather round, I've got some words to spin. And trust me, it's not your garden-variety self-help tale of "rise at the crack of dawn, meditate till you're floating or dine on kale for breakfast." No, this book is a juicy and refreshing slice of life that'll hopefully have you smiling, nodding like a Churchill dog, and maybe even shedding a tear.

Before we dive headfirst into this glorious rollercoaster of a book, it would be an excellent opportunity to introduce myself. I'm Jack. I am naturally inclined to observe and contemplate life's complexities like a Jigsaw puzzle. I'm an activator, driven to get things done, and my strengths lie in empathy, strategy, and effective communication. I've been fortunate to grow up in a loving family, work on exciting projects, have great friends, travel to incredible places, and maintain good health. However, I'm far from perfect. I'm impulsive, impatient and tend to get bored very easily, so I'm not writing this book from a place of superiority - far from it. I'm also not writing this book from a place of authorship – trust me, I'm no JK Rowling. This book is about sharing thoughts and stories, hoping you might find something relatable or thought-provoking along the way.

Let me set the scene. We're smack dab in the middle of the roaring twenties, the 2020s, a time when information rains down upon us like confetti at a New Year's bash. The other day, I stumbled upon a 20-second TikTok tutorial on how to clean my air fryer. Who knew cleaning could be so exciting?

Thanks to streaming apps Netflix and Spotify, we've got more movies and tunes at our fingertips than we know what to do with. We can stream stories that tickle our fancy and melodies that make our hearts dance. And let's not forget the magic of social media — Facebook, X, LinkedIn, BeReal; you name it — they've turned us into global voyeurs, granting us a front-row seat to the chronicles of our fellow citizens.

We've also become more conscious of the gremlins called racism and inequality, and we're taking steps— albeit slow and stumbling —to sculpt a world that's a little fairer. More people are waking up to these issues, peeling back the layers of ignorance like an onion. Sure, the UK's seen a surge in race-related incidents over the years, but could we be better at spotting the bad apples now? More BAME (Black, Asian, Minority Ethnic) folks are marching into universities, and women are storming the castles of power with sledgehammers - smashing their way through the glass ceilings.

Disabled people are finding their place in the workforce, fewer souls are struggling beneath the poverty line, and as I pen these words, employment numbers are soaring. At the same time, job vacancies pile up like discarded wrapping paper on Christmas morning. The LGBTQ+ community is winning more rights than ever before, and their rainbow flags aren't just fluttering in June; they're a year-round spectacle.

But, and there's always a "but" in life, isn't there? Despite all this progress, we're witnessing a spike in gloomy societal behaviours. Depression? It's knocking on doors like a Jehovah's Witness, and countless folks are turning to pills to tame that dark beast within. Anxiety? It's become the uninvited guest at life's party, crashing celebrations with its nervous energy. Suicides? Still happening, and it breaks our hearts. Stress? Oh, it's not in short supply.

One fine day, not too long ago, I did one of my favourite pastimes—people-watching. I plopped my arse down, slipped in my Air Pods, cranked up some classical tunes, and just observed. It got me thinking: why does our society seem like a compass gone haywire in an era of unparalleled comforts and opportunities?

So, as the clock struck midnight on the eve of 2023, I hatched a resolution—not to master the art of productivity or wave a wand to fix the world's woes, but to read. To read more and understand why our society seems to have misplaced its North Star. Every morning, I'd dive into news articles and self-help books, dissecting the world's quirks and how humans are advised to surf the tsunami of life's challenges.

And here's the kicker: amid the chorus of self-help serenades, we've become obsessed with optimisation, efficiency, and the wild goose chase of perfection. Most books I've read in recent times have been authored by people who have had fascinating and extraordinary things happen in their lives. It's like listening to advice from folks who've scaled Mount Everest blindfolded or read the Davinci code before breakfast. I'm not knocking them, but it's a tad challenging to relate. It's as if we're in perpetual pursuit of a superhuman version of ourselves.

But what if the secret to a fulfilling life isn't about becoming some fantastical superhuman? What if it's about kicking off those high heels of comparison, ditching the relentless quest for success, and stopping our futile attempts at keeping up with the Joneses (or Kardashians, if that's your jam)? We're drowning in an ocean of self-improvement mantras in our modern world. We're told to optimise, maximise, and revolutionise our lives until we're the Michael Jordan of existence.

But what if the key to a satisfying life lies not in trying to become something we're not? What if it's about finding joy in the everyday, spotting beauty in our imperfections, and digging up wisdom from those mundane moments that sprinkle life with joy? What if it's about Getting Over Ourselves , our fixation with perfection, and our relentless pursuit of Instagrammable moments?

So, I set out on a quest to pen a book and christened it "Get Over Yourself ." Here's the plot twist: I don't intend to plunge headfirst into the abyss of self-help that promises to transform you into a productivity guru, yoga teacher, or the next Greta Thunberg. I wanted something different — something deliciously human. So, brace yourselves; you won't find groundbreaking revelations on these pages. You'll likely nod your head, maybe crack a smile, or perhaps even have an "a-ha!" moment that grounds you back on good old planet Earth. Or, who knows, you might read this book and think, "Well, what a load of shite!" I hope you don't, but if, at any point, you find yourself nodding or grinning, I've done what I set out to do.

Within these pages, you won't stumble upon a 10-step master plan to unlock the universe's most profound mysteries. Instead, you'll uncover ten refreshers — short, snappy chapters that'll make you exclaim, "Bloody hell, I've been there too!" These chapters are gentle reminders; the whispers often drowned out by the racket of our bustling lives. You'll find some food for thought questions at the end of each chapter. Once you've reached the end of each chapter, I want to encourage you to snack away at the food for thought questions I've written and have a good think about your answers. I also challenge you to ask someone else these questions – whether it be a colleague, partner, parent, or sibling. Let's have some healthy discussion!

So, if you're game for an optimistic, amusing, and slightly cheeky voyage of self-discovery to Get Over Yourself , turn that page. Let's embark on a journey to unearth the joy that's been napping in plain sight. Fasten your seatbelt - it's about to get good!

CHAPTER 1
ENJOY THE MOMENT

"THE JOY YOU SEEK IS NOT IN THE FUTURE OR THE PAST; IT'S IN THE EXQUISITE MELODY OF TODAY."

Ronan Keating once said: *Life is a Rollercoaster, Just gotta ride it.* He's right. Life is like a fantastic roller coaster ride, and memories are the snapshots we take while zipping through the twists, turns, and loop-de-loops.

Memories are like the glittering treasures you collect along the journey - the high-fives with friends, the spontaneous adventures, and the belly laughs that echo through time. Each memory is a dazzling gem, and you, my friend, are the master jeweller crafting a unique, sparkling necklace of experiences.

But here's the plot twist – don't get so caught up in curating that necklace that you forget to ride the roller coaster! Sometimes, we're so busy trying to capture the perfect moment that we miss the thrill of the live show happening right before our eyes.

Now say **CHEESE** because in the early 1800s, a superb and very clever French inventor decided to revolutionise how people see and save their favourite moments. Instead of painting pictures, he used light and chemicals. He started playing with an old-school device now known as a camera obscura. He put a plate near his window with bitumen placed onto it - leaving it to soak up the sun. Bitumen is a thick, black petroleum product derived from crude oil. It is widely used in construction for its adhesive and waterproofing properties, particularly in asphalt for roads and pavements. After lots of trial and error, bam! In 1826, he snapped the world's first pic—a blurry view from his window in Burgundy, the wine region in France.

But the real magic happened in 1839 when the French inventor teamed up with a mate, and they unveiled the daguerreotype process. It used shiny copper sheets and some mercury magic to make detailed pics that lasted forever. 1839 was also the year the first-ever selfie was taken - who would have thought? Photography went from 0-60 at the speed of a shutter sound.

Everybody went mad for it! Photo studios popped up everywhere, and people could finally get their faces captured on these tiny metal plates. And that's how photography crashed the party of modern society.

As the years passed, photography got fancier. Glass plates, wet-plate thingies, and a guy named George Eastman invented roll film, making cameras more incredible and accessible. The Kodak Brownie in 1900 made everyone a photography pro - giving everyone that 'Kodak Moment.'

Fast forward to the 1900s, and tech got wild. First, we had disposable cameras you had to wait forever to develop - remember them? Polaroids? Shake it like you mean it! Then came digital cameras and smartphones, turning everyone into a snapaholic. Now, it's easier than ever to incorporate photography into everyday life.

Today, in the 21st century, the camera is a mega part of our super cool and diverse society! It's not just a tool for taking pics; it's a storytelling champ and a communication method. Check out Instagram and Facebook – they're bursting with pics that catch life's wild moments, big and small.

In this digital age, cameras are everywhere – in our pockets and gadgets. They're how we show off our lives, capture history doing its thing, and let our creative vibes flow. The evolution of the camera has made everyone a photo pro, turning us into story-tellers and low-key artists. It's still changing how we see things, capturing the spirit of our modern world one click at a time. But hey, is it all good vibes? Right?

Modern life is a dazzling battlefield where distractions, es-pecially the digital kind, throw a relentless party! **Picture this:** a world saturated with technology, where smartphones, tablets, and computers play a symphony of pings, notifications, emails, and social media updates, all competing for the crown of our attention. These devices are like mischievous imps, tempting us with quick hits of information and fun, turning resistance into a Herculean task.

Contributing to the chaotic nature of contemporary life, the work environment has transformed us into jugglers, attempting to balance an excessive number of tasks simultaneously. This has led to a blurred distinction between our professional and per-sonal lives. Thanks to the wonders of remote work and digital tools galore, many of us are practically glued to our screens all day, every day. It's like being tethered to a digital rollercoaster, where work tasks, personal messages, and digital delights are all fighting each other for the front seat at our show of attention. And hold onto your hat because here comes the temptation to multitask, the grand illusionist of productivity! People are at-tempting a high-wire act, juggling multiple responsibilities like a plate-spinner on steroids. But, spoiler alert, instead of boost-ing our focus and productivity, it's more like a circus act gone wrong, leaving us scattered and struggling to keep all the balls in the air. The result? A decrease in our ability to stay on point and get things done.

Beyond digital distractions, there are numerous other distractions in modern life, including the noise and commotion of urban environments, the allure of television and streaming services, and the constant bombardment of advertising and marketing messages. The fast pace of life and the prevalence of information overload contribute to a general sense of restlessness and difficulty maintaining sustained attention. As a result, resisting distractions and staying fully engaged in the present moment has become an increasingly challenging endeavour in our modern society.

All of the pictures, videos, Instagram posts, pings, and notifications led me to ask myself a question. How often do we just Enjoy The Moment these days?

In British homes, a surprising six out of ten meals are now enjoyed in front of the television. A study published in Psychological Science discovered that individuals who engaged in mental tasks or watched TV at the same time as eating were more likely to perceive their food as bland. It's like attending a flavour party where the DJ is on mute. When you focus on a screen, your taste buds miss out on the fantastic taste parade happening in your mouth. The distraction phenomenon isn't just restricted to picturesque places in the world you visit; it extends to the comforts of your own home, when you're in your pyjamas, tucking into a wholesome dinner.

It's not just our taste buds that are influenced by TV and music. The 2020 pandemic brought a significant shift in work routines, especially for those accustomed to a daily commute to the office. Admittedly, like many others, I fell into a bit of a lazier routine when i started to work from home.

My mornings now involve a 20-minute walk along the canal to a local café to grab a coffee. One day, I woke up to the dreaded realisation that my phone hadn't charged overnight, sparking a moment of anxiety. Surprisingly, this turned out to be a blessing in disguise. It nudged me to embrace the moment during my morning walk without the distraction of my phone and headphones. Leaving them at home allowed me to truly absorb the beauty around me – the chirping birds, the gentle flow of the water, the vibrant wildlife, and the changing colours of the trees. It became a lesson in appreciating the beauty right on my doorstep, emphasising the importance of being present and discovering the tranquillity that comes with it.

Have you ever experienced a "hell yeah!" moment when something extraordinary happens, like a spontaneous flash mob or a random train serenade that gets everyone grooving? Initially, you're thrilled by the great moment, but do you stop there, soaking in the goodness, or do you find yourself reaching for your phone, eager to capture the magic and end up watching the entire event through a tiny screen?

Here's my personal pet peeve: standing at a compact 5ft 7, I can't help but be irritated when someone in front of me at a crowded concert is recording the entire thing on their mobile phone. Will anyone really care to watch a video of a distant figure singing on stage? Will they ever revisit that video? The likely answer is... probably not. Such video clips often end up in the digital graveyard on your camera roll, joining the thousands of pictures of people's meals that were snapped while the delicious food they ordered went cold. Let's be honest with ourselves: how often do we actually look back at pictures of our meals?

It's become increasingly apparent in our modern society that we're struggling to savour the simple beauty of the present moment. Instead of fully immersing ourselves in the now, we often prioritise capturing and sharing our experiences through the lens of our smartphones. This shift in behaviour reflects several underlying factors that have reshaped how we engage with the world around us.

One driving force behind this phenomenon is the omnipresence of digital technology. The advent of smartphones and social media platforms has placed a miniature camera and a direct line to the virtual world in our pockets. The ease of snapping photos or shooting videos has made documenting our lives a breeze. The promise of instant gratification in the form of likes, comments, and shares on social media has turned the act of capturing moments into a compelling habit.

Also, the concept of "FOMO" or "Fear of Missing Out" has taken root in our digital age. In a world where everyone's highlights are accessible on our screens, we've become anxious about not being part of the action or missing a shareable moment - even though it might not be a moment you want to be part of. This fear drives us to pre-emptively document our experiences to prove to ourselves and others that we were present and accounted for.

The pressure to curate an idealised version of our lives for the virtual audience has led to what some call "the Instagram effect." We're inclined to capture only the most picturesque, exciting, or curated aspects of our lives, leaving behind the less photogenic, mundane, yet equally valuable moments. This constant pursuit of picture-perfect moments can inadvertently rob us of the genuine and unfiltered experiences that make life rich and authentic.

There's also a growing sense of validation tied to social media metrics. The number of likes, comments, and shares serves as a digital scoreboard, and many of us have become unwitting participants in this online popularity contest. We prioritise capturing moments that are most likely to get attention, sometimes at the expense of our personal enjoyment of those moments.

In this age of digital documentation, we find ourselves at a crossroads. While technology offers us incredible ways to connect and share our lives, it also challenges our ability to fully engage with the present. To break free from this trend and rediscover the joy of being in the moment, we must re-strike a balance between our digital lives and the world unfolding before our very eyes.

Allow me to recount a memorable visit to the marvellous Leaning Tower of Pisa, nestled in the charming city of Pisa – a fact that seems almost self-evident. Before I delve into the details, I must candidly admit to my hypocrisy. Yes, I joined the ranks of those tourists who got their friends to capture various poses, pretending to push, lean on, and kick over the world-renowned tower.

Yet, upon reflection, I asked myself a question. The Leaning Tower of Pisa stands as a universally acknowledged architectural gem. Everyone knows what it looks like. So, why did I squander time partaking in these antics alongside numerous other tourists that day instead of living in the moment with a cornetto or a refreshing Bierre Moretti in hand? It seems like a peculiar impulse to capture well-known landmarks in such clichéd ways - right?

What if I were to propose that the version of myself enjoying a cornetto and sipping Bierre Moretti would retain more details, appreciate more beauty, and acquire more knowledge about the Leaning Tower of Pisa compared to the version that fancied myself as Italy's next top model? Yep - it's true!

Picture of me being one of them annoying tourists just out-side the **Leaning Tower Of Pisa** *in Italy*

The phenomenon of "offloading" memory through photography is known as the photo-taking impairment effect. Linda Henkel, a psychology professor at Fairfield University, explains that when individuals rely on technology to capture a moment, they essentially delegate the task of remembering to the camera. Consequently, they may not fully engage with the experience, diminishing their ability to remember it.

To illustrate, if you write down someone's phone number, your brain may signal there's no need to commit it to memory because the information is documented. This convenience, however, becomes apparent when the written information is no longer accessible. Henkel initially examined this effect in 2013 and demonstrated that individuals had difficulty recalling art objects from a museum when taking pictures of them. Subsequent studies in 2017 and 2021 have replicated these findings.

Not remembering the details - it's what happens when we're distracted by the process of taking a photo, how we hold our phone, framing the shot to make sure people are smiling, and the background is to our liking, ensuring the image isn't blurry — all of which uses up cognitive skills or attentional resources that could otherwise help us encode or retain that memory.

Sadly, attentional disengagement is especially likely to occur during milestone moments, such as when you attend a graduation or when a child blows out birthday candles. Those are times when we have the added pressure of capturing a magical moment and concentrating on getting it right. Our brains are caught up in helping us take that perfect photo instead of retaining that perfect memory.

Imagine you're caught up in playing photographer. In that case, you might end up with a killer shot to prove you were somewhere nice, but the memory might be as elusive as trying to find the TV remote in the dark. Compare that with a more extended visit where you're only mildly distracted initially, snapping one or two pics. That's the recipe for a memory. Sure, many folks savour the moment before unleashing their inner paparazzo, and that's awesome. You might be reading this, rolling your eyes and thinking, "Don't patronise me!" But let's face it, we've all been there in this camera-happy age. As I mentioned at the get-go of this book, consider it a friendly nudge – just refreshing what we already know!

If someone, like me, suggests you're sacrificing meaningful memories to boost your social media image on platforms with little importance to your followers, pause and reflect. Does this statement evoke any emotions for you?

Let's shift gears and consider the counterargument. Photography isn't just about selfies and scenic shots; it's a powerhouse for storytelling. Through visual narratives, we can articulate our perspectives and emotions, turning a mundane moment into a captivating tale. It's a means of self-expression, a therapeutic outlet letting us delve into and comprehend our feelings.

Also, photographs aren't just pixels; they're time capsules. They immortalise cultural, social, and personal milestones, creating a visual archive of our history. These snapshots combine individual journeys and capture collective experiences, contributing to a richer understanding of our shared past. Those vintage photographs are like time machines, allowing younger generations to step into the shoes of their ancestors – understanding the wars fought, the fashion trends, the cars on the road, and the traditions that used to be fulfilled. This side of photography fosters a sense of continuity, stitching together the fabric of connection across generations.

Despite my occasional grumble about the social media scene, let's remember it's a global fiesta where you can connect with all sorts of characters and give diverse voices a stage. Last year, I decided to take on a triathlon whilst rocking a pair of man tits and zero motivation for training. I stumbled across a Facebook group for Triathlon beginners, and guess what? It was a spectacle of regular folks, just like me, flaunting their triathlon victories worldwide. I'm talking dad bods conquering triathlons left, right, and centre! I'd look at their snaps and think, "Well, if they can smash it, so can I?" The contagious vibes created this positivity snowball that nudged everyone to display the highs and lows of their triathlon journey.

Now, let's rewind to what I spoke about earlier in this chapter. Are the photos you're scrolling through genuine moments of pure joy, or are they a staged production, heavily seasoned with filters like Clarendon or Juno, and tweaked to make the moment seem fancier than it was? Hold that thought; we'll dig deeper into this rabbit hole later in the book.

In essence, the purpose and benefits of taking pictures are multifaceted, encompassing personal, social, and cultural dimensions, and the positive impact extends far beyond the immediate act of capturing an image. But in modern-day life, we must ask ourselves why people are taking pictures. Is it so they remember the moment or to show off the moment to other people?

- Enjoying the moment and being present gives a range of benefits. It can temporarily set aside worries about the past or future, leading to lower stress levels.

- Mindfulness, or being fully engaged in the present, has been linked to better mental well-being, reduced anxiety, and improved mood.

- Being present in interactions, we build stronger connections with others. It fosters better communication and empathy.

- Enjoying life's moments, big or small, gives us a sense of gratitude for the simple joys in life, encouraging a more positive outlook.

- Being fully in the moment allows us to fully experience and appreciate the sights, sounds, and sensations around us, enriching our overall sensory experience.

- Immersing in the situation often sparks creativity, as your mind is free to explore and make novel connections without the distraction of past or future thoughts.

- Living in the now can positively affect physical health, including lowered blood pressure and improved immune function.

When we immerse ourselves in the present, we break free from the shackles of overthinking and self-judgment. The moment is a canvas waiting for our vibrant strokes, inviting us to be fully alive and unburdened by the weight of ego. To Get Over Ourselves, we must first get into the rhythm of the moment – to dance with the spontaneity of life, revel in the beauty of the now, and discover the extraordinary within the ordinary. It's a journey towards self-liberation, and the destination is a place where joy, authenticity, and a profound sense of self await.

Let's casually stroll down memory lane and appreciate some of the cool stuff we've seen in recent years. Nowadays, the younger generation is all about capturing those picture-perfect moments, jazzing them up, and sharing them on social media in a flash. It's become a timing game, with people strategically dropping posts at just the right time for that extra engagement boost. But, beneath the social media hustle, there's a more profound mission – shaking off a bit of that self-centred vibe. We all love a good thumbs-up or a nice comment; it's like a little ego boost that keeps us coming back for more. So, maybe it's time to step back, enjoy the moment, and share the spotlight.

You're not just on this earth to exist; you're here to truly live and embrace each moment as a precious gift. It's hard to let go of the past's weight and the future's uncertainties, but if we do, we allow the beauty of the present to wash over us like a gentle wave. Enjoying the moment is a rebellion against the chaos of distraction and a commitment to lapping up the richness of our experiences. It's about finding joy in the simplest things – a warm embrace, good humour, or the sun glowing on your face.

Indulging in the present isn't just a feel-good vibe; it's a game-changer. You know the saying, 'Everything in moderation'? Well, consider it the concrete pillars that hold this book together – and for good reason. Snap those pictures until your camera begs for mercy, showcase them to the world, but here's the golden rule: in the midst of your camera-clicking extravaganza and all the distractions that life throws at us, wherever you find yourself, whatever adventure unfolds – make 'enjoying the moment' your top priority. Embrace the now and let your zest for life shine through! Grab hold of each moment because, let's face it, most opportunities don't knock twice.

Enjoy The Moment

FOOD FOR THOUGHT QUESTIONS ...

1) In the past few weeks, how often did you find yourself genuinely present in the moment without the distraction of capturing it on your phone?

2) Consider a cherished memory. How would your recollection of that moment differ if you had chosen to experience it without technological interruptions?

CHAPTER 2
SAY FUCK IT REGULARLY

"SAY 'FUCK IT' AND WATCH THE EXTRAORDINARY UNFOLD. EMBRACE SPONTANEITY, DEFY NORMS, AND LET THE MAGIC HAPPEN."

In the pulsating beat of our daily lives, there emerges a chapter that echoes with the spirit of rebellion and spontaneity – the chapter titled "Say F*ck It More Often." In these pages, we'll unravel the art of calculated audacity, explore its tangible benefits through real-life examples, and weigh the merits of this exhilarating approach against the grounding wisdom of moderation.

The heartbeat of our existence often follows a familiar rhythm - work, eat, sleep, repeat. It's a pattern etched into the fabric of our lives. Routines, with their comforting predictability, offer a sense of stability and familiarity. Yet, amid the mundane hum of our daily tasks, there's a bellowing call from that voice in our head to break free from the handcuffs of routine and embrace the unscripted scenes that will play out before us.

Before delving into the world of spontaneity, let's pay homage to the merits of routine. Regular sleep patterns, consistent meals, and habitual activities contribute to physical and mental well-being. The stability of routine organises our days, preventing the overwhelming sea of chaos that can accompany a lack of structure.

Consider this: If we spend over 70% of our week working and approximately 65% of our lives on the job between the ages of 18 and 65, what room does that leave for spontaneity? How often do we throw caution to the wind and shout, "Fuck It"?

The average Brit does 13,000 laundry washes in their lifetime. We fold and iron nearly 9000 shirts in our lifetime and lose 756 socks - an integral part of the laundry process. We take out the bins, mow the lawn, change the beds, wash the windows, clean the dishes, mop the floors and vacuum more than our Henry Hoovers could have ever imagined. We do all this while balancing the demands of working, family, keeping fit and trying to have a healthy social life.

The term "Fuck It" might be unfamiliar to some, but its essence is universal. It's the rebellious declaration that sometimes, rules and routines need to take a back seat. It's similar to saying, "Take the plunge," "Risk it all," or "Throw caution to the wind." These expressions encompass a willingness to embrace uncertainty to face potential consequences head-on.

Spontaneity has profound implications for our pursuit of happiness and personal fulfilment. Picture this: Captivated by a sudden burst of sunshine, you and your friends decide to pack up the car for an impromptu road trip to the beach. The spontaneity of the decision infuses the journey with excitement and adventure.

Or imagine a lazy Sunday afternoon with the family transforming into a spontaneous day out, the decision made on a whim leading to an exhilarating experience etched into the memory of everyone who took the plunge and joined in.

On a tedious weekday, you and your other half decide to try

out a new restaurant and catch a movie, turning a routine day into a much-needed evening of quality time.

Or the most relatable of them all, you've had a proper shit week at work, you go for a casual drink, and you end with dancing like a nutter, snogging a random stranger on the dancefloor before swinging by a kebab shop and stumbling home.

Do any of these sound familiar? If you're nodding or smiling because the memories are flooding back to you - take a moment of reflection. How did those moments of madness make you feel? Who were you with, and what did you get from it?

Understanding why we remember happy moments involves a mix of brain activities. When something joyful happens, certain brain parts get more active. Chemicals like dopamine and serotonin help make these good memories stronger. They go through changes in the brain that build stronger connections, especially in the prefrontal cortex, which helps us remember our life story. Remembering happy times is influenced by how we felt at the time, making positive memories easier to remember. Chemicals like dopamine, linked to feeling good, play a big part in making sure we remember these happy moments. Another chemical, oxytocin, comes into play when we're bonding socially, making those positive social memories stick. And remember, sharing experiences and having strong social bonds also help make happy memories. So, in simple terms, the science of happy memories is like understanding how our brain deals with all the good stuff that makes our lives better.

These moments, born from saying "Fuck It," have a unique flavour, a distinct zest that breaks the 'same shit, different day mantra' that we find ourselves saying more than ever before.

Studies reveal spontaneity isn't just about creating exciting moments; it positively impacts our mental well-being. Research from the American Psychological Association suggests that engaging in spontaneous activities can elevate our mood and reduce the feeling of being stressed. When we relinquish the need for absolute control, allowing ourselves to step away from constant planning, our minds find freedom. This liberation contributes to a more relaxed and content state, boosting mental resilience and emotional well-being - which has a knock-on impact on everything else we do in life.

Spontaneity isn't confined to personal joy; it extends its influence into professional and personal growth. A study from the Harvard Business Review highlights that professionals who occasionally take calculated risks, such as reaching out to influential figures without a predefined agenda, often expand their networks significantly. Moreover, spontaneous experiences become lasting memories that contribute to a sense of life satisfaction and a profound sense of fulfilment.

The allure of spontaneity lies in its ability to break away from the ordinary, to infuse life with unpredictability. However, like everything in life, it requires a balanced approach. Everything in moderation, as they say! Too much spontaneity can lead to overspending, accidents, and missed opportunities. It may have the complete opposite effect.

For example, if you said 'Fuck It' every time someone asked you to go to the pub - you'd be ploughing hundreds and hundreds of pounds into the tills of your local boozers, feeling hungover most of the time whilst your physical and mental health takes a pounding. If you say 'To Hell With It' every time you see a cream cake, you'll lose that feeling of treating yourself.

The key lies in thoughtful spontaneity—a conscious mix of seizing opportunities and considering risks. It's about finding the sweet spot where unpredictability coexists with an illusion of order. Thoughtful spontaneity is not about impulsive decision-making but a proactive and informed approach to shaping our path, aligning with our values and goals.

While spontaneity injects excitement into life, it's crucial to acknowledge potential downsides. Financially, impromptu decisions can lead to overspending, with studies showing a link between impulsivity and financial stress.

I'm no stranger to this tale. In early 2015, my mates Ruman, Joe, and Dan pitched the idea of a three-month escapade around the world, a chance to break free from the daily grind. Despite being at the dawn of our professional lives, the opportunity was too enticing to resist.

We had 6 months to meticulously planned, save, and co-ordinate our sabbaticals with our employers. However, reality hit me like a ton of bricks when, 10 weeks before take-off, I realised I had saved absolutely nothing. Nada. I was about to embark on a global adventure without a pot to piss in. So, in a moment of audacity, I applied for a loan from a supermarket bank, spinning a few tales about a steady income and home improvements. Surprisingly, they approved the loan, and suddenly, a hefty sum landed in my bank account, paving the way for months of living my best life.

Accepting the invitation to travel became a defining 'Fuck It' moment, and I have no regrets. Yet, hindsight is a beautiful guide. If only I had saved before the journey, those years of post-travel debt repayment might have been unnecessary. The monthly loan deductions did bring financial stress, but in the grand scheme of things, I have no regrets. Travelling taught me so much. However, a more calculated approach could have meant not just a memorable adventure but also the possibility of coming home to new wheels or a place of my own.

*Picture of a tweet I sent to Sainsburys bank as a laugh. Living it up in **Thailand** after telling them the loan was for home improvements.*

In professional contexts, poorly considered spontaneous decisions can have negative repercussions. Psychologically, some individuals may find spontaneity stressful, especially those who prefer structure and predictability. Relationships, too, can be strained if spontaneous decisions are not communicated well, as your other half may not appreciate you randomly saying YOLO (you only live once) and bringing home a cat that you brought from Mick down the pub.

While spontaneity can be invigorating, finding a balance with thoughtful planning is essential. The careful interplay between calculated risks and responsible liberation ensures that spontaneity enhances our lives without causing unnecessary disruptions.

Now it's time to tug on those heartstrings of yours. There are two things in life that every single human being on this planet experiences. You live, and you sadly die. Everyone has known someone in their life who sadly went before their time. And what does this tell us? It tells us that life is precious, unpredictable and short.

When people say, "Life's too short," they basically remind us that our time on Earth is limited. It's like a little nudge to encourage us to focus on what really matters and enjoy life. The idea is not to get bogged down by minor problems but to embrace the good stuff — like spending good quality time with our nearest and dearest, doing the things we love, and having adventures. It's a reminder to live authentically, be true to ourselves, and not waste time on things that don't bring us joy.

As we navigate the complexities of life, let spontaneity be our guide —a key to unlocking a world of joy, resilience, and fulfilment. As we make our way through life, the anthem of saying 'Fuck It' resonates a rebellious melody inviting us to waltz in the spontaneity of the present.

This chapter has been a journey through the vibrant landscapes of unpredictability, where joy unfolds in the spaces where caution is cast aside. Yet, amid the celebration of unfettered spontaneity, let's gently hold a mirror before our daily lives. Are we maestros of our own orchestration, conducting the spirited tempo of spontaneity, or have we unwittingly given in to the seductive lull of routine?

In this moment of reflection, let's ponder the balance —a harmonious dance between responsibility and audacity. Saying 'Fuck It' is not an endorsement of being reckless; instead, it's a call to responsible liberation. It encourages us to seize the moment with an open heart, shatter the chains of routine, and paint the canvas of life we want to paint.

Welcoming spontaneity and just saying 'Fuck It' more often is a game-changer in the whole process of "Getting Over Ourselves." It's like breaking free from the daily grind and routine that usually holds us back. Taking those spontaneous leaps helps us grow personally and toughens us up in the face of life's curveballs. It's about discovering parts of ourselves we didn't know existed and letting our creative juices flow. Saying 'Fuck It' becomes a badge of freedom, letting us live authentically and embrace the crazy twists of life.

What's more, it takes away the fear of messing up, teaching us that failures are just stepping stones. Beyond the psychology, it's a mood-lifter, making our lives more positive and rewarding. So, by letting spontaneity grab the wheel, we break free from societal norms, live real, be real and find joy in the unexpected moments that make our journey uniquely ours.

Consider this not a conclusion but a beginning —a starting point for a life made with memories and experiences. The responsible rebel within us yearns to break free, to step into the unknown with a sprinkle of caution, creating stories that your grandchildren will laugh about. No matter how big or small, I challenge you to take the plunge, be audacious and say those two words that will unlock opportunity and hopefully put a smile on your face.

FOOD FOR THOUGHT QUESTIONS ...

1) Recall a time when you embraced spontaneity. How did it impact your mood, and what did you learn from that experience?

2) What routines or habits do you feel are constraining your sense of freedom and adventure? How can you break out of them?

3) Identify a passion or interest you've been putting off pursuing. How can you inject a bit of madness into your routine to make room for it?

CHAPTER 3
BE GLASS HALF FULL

"CHOOSE TO SEE THE GLASS AS HALF FULL, AND SUDDENLY EVERY CHALLENGE BECOMES AN OPPORTUNITY, EVERY SETBACK A STEPPING STONE, AND EVERY MOMENT A GIFT WAITING TO BE UNWRAPPED."

In our weird, wonderful, and busy lives, we often find ourselves standing at the crossroads of perception, faced with the age-old question: Is the glass half full or half empty? In the following few pages, we'll embark on a journey through the realms of optimism, realism, and the delicate dance between them in our quest to unveil the wonders of "Being Glass Half Full."

Picture this: After a marathon day at work, you stumble through the front door – kicking off your shoes and chucking your bag to the floor. You shuffle into the kitchen, swinging open the fridge or turning on the tap – pouring your favourite drink into a glass. Its contents are level, resting at the midpoint of the glass. **Do you see this glass as half full or half empty?**

Some see it as an abundance waiting to be appreciated— half full, a reservoir of potential. Others, however, might cast a doubtful eye, fixating on what's absent—half empty, a drink with perceived limitations.

The "glass half full vs. glass half empty" scenario is often framed as a paradox. A paradox typically involves a situation where contradictory elements or ideas coexist, leading to logical or conceptual difficulties.

In the case of the "glass half full vs. glass half empty" metaphor, the content of the glass remains constant—the glass is both half full and half empty simultaneously. The apparent paradox arises from people's contrasting perspectives or interpretations regarding the same situation.

While the specific origin may not be traceable, the metaphor has become a part of our everyday language. The phrase often illustrates differing outlooks on life and attitudes towards challenges. Some view the glass as half full, emphasising what's present and expressing optimism, while others see it as half empty, focusing on what's lacking and reflecting a more pessimistic viewpoint.

As we delve into the debate, let's first acknowledge the merits of the Glass Half Empty perspective. A dash of scepticism, a hint of realism—it's the practical lens that can help us navigate the pitfalls and uncertainties of life. In emptiness lies the chance for spotting opportunities that may be obscured in the dazzle of unrestrained optimism.

There are many things to rightly have a dose of pessimism about. Economic challenges like job insecurity and income inequality can contribute to a more pessimistic outlook. These concerns about personal and financial well-being can shape individuals' perceptions of the overall state of society. Modern society faces significant global challenges, including climate change, political unrest, and public health crises. These complex issues can contribute to uncertainty and pessimism about our future. Societal divisions, whether political, cultural, or social, can create an atmosphere of tension and negativity. Perceptions of societal discord can lead to a belief that the glass is more empty than full. There's also rising awareness of environmental issues, which, while crucial for fostering positive change, can contribute to a sense of pessimism about the state of the planet and the future.

During daily life, individuals often encounter setbacks ranging from job-related challenges, such as unexpected unemployment and workplace conflicts, to relationship struggles, including breakups and family disputes. Health issues, both physical and mental, financial strains, academic or career setbacks, and grief from loss are familiar facets of life. Legal troubles, friendship changes, personal rejections, and failures in personal pursuits also contribute to life's complexities. Resilience is crucial in facing these challenges. We adapt, we learn, and we persist despite adversities.

However, despite all of the challenges we face in life, are we striking a delicate balance between optimism and realism that transforms challenges into triumphs? The Glass Half Empty perspective becomes a compass, guiding us through the maze of uncertainty with a discerning eye.

Over time, the "Glass Half Full" metaphor has found its way into discussions about resilience, mental attitude, and the impact of optimism on overall well-being. It's a versatile expression that resonates in various aspects of life, from personal philosophy to motivational discussions and even in marketing and advertising to convey positive messaging.

Optimism acts as a shield against the storms of life, offering resilience in times of challenge. It fuels the engine of perseverance, turning setbacks into stepping stones for growth. When we embrace optimism, we open ourselves to a world of possibilities, where hurdles become opportunities and difficulties become catalysts for change and growth.

But what other positives does being glass half full have? It gives us a sense of resilience for all the challenges that life can throw at us! A Glass Half Full perspective fosters resilience, empowering individuals to bounce back from setbacks with a positive outlook and unwavering determination.

It's also great for our health! Various scientific studies suggest that an optimistic mindset is associated with lower stress levels, better immune function, and improved physical health, contributing to a longer, more vibrant life. Optimists are better equipped to manage stress. Their ability to focus on solutions rather than dwelling on problems helps alleviate stressors, promoting mental and emotional well-being. A Glass Half Full perspective fuels motivation and ambition. Optimists are more likely to set and pursue ambitious goals - fitness or non-fitness-related! But that motivation to live a healthier life, getting out there and doing things can help overcome obstacles and achieve success. Humour, our trusty companion on this journey, also deserves a spotlight. Life's absurdities become more bearable when viewed through a comedic lens. It's a coping mechanism, a shield against the arrows of negativity, and a reminder that even in the darkest moments, a spark of laughter can illuminate the path forward. And we all know that laughter is life's best medicine.

Being glass half full is also helpful at work. There is always that one negative nelly at work. Even though sometimes it's hard to remain positive amongst the pigeons at work - being glass half full helps us innovate, adapt to situations and build better relationships with our colleagues. Positivity acts as a catalyst for creativity, unlocking out-of-the-box thinking and problem-solving abilities. Optimists tend to develop stronger interpersonal connections. Their positive energy is contagious, fostering a harmonious environment and attracting like-minded individuals into their lives. Positive thinkers are more adaptable to change. They approach new situations with an open mind, seeing possibilities rather than obstacles, making them more agile in navigating life's twists and turns.

Perceptions of whether modern society leans towards a "Glass Half Empty" or "Glass Half Full" mindset can vary, and the characterisation of society as more pessimistic may be influenced by several factors. Let's talk about the news. Negative news attracts more attention, and media outlets often prioritise sensational or adverse stories. Constant exposure to such content can contribute to a perception that the world is more negative than positive.

Rolling news and social media algorithms contribute to increased pessimism by fostering selective exposure and negative bias. These algorithms prioritise content aligning with users' beliefs, creating echo chambers reinforcing negative perspectives. The constant exposure to negative news and divisive content, coupled with a lack of balance in positive information, can lead to a skewed and pessimistic worldview.

In today's world, our addiction to news is fuelled by the constant stream of information through news apps on our devices. The allure lies in staying informed about global events. This addiction is evident even on slow news days, where the hunger for updates persists.

A historical event that always makes me chuckle is when UK Prime Minister Harold Macmillan once faced a lone BBC reporter at an airport upon returning from a foreign affairs trip. When asked if he had anything to share, Macmillan, consulting his Foreign Secretary, responded with a resolute "No." The reporter, accepting this lack of news, gracefully thanked the Prime

Minister.

In similar fashion, on 18th April 1930, the BBC's news announcer found themselves in an unusual situation as they stepped up to the microphone with a surprising message: "There is no news." This unexpected revelation became the entirety of the script for the 20:45 news bulletin. Following this unprecedented statement, piano music gracefully filled the airwaves, providing an intriguing backdrop for the remaining 15-minute segment. It's bonkers to think of switching on Sky News today, only to hear the melody of piano music and not a single drop of news.

The concept of 24-hour news channels started to take shape in the 1980s. One of the pioneers in this field was CNN (Cable News Network), which launched on June 1, 1980. CNN, founded by Ted Turner, was the first television channel to provide news coverage 24 hours a day.

The idea of a 24-hour news channel was ground breaking at the time, as traditional news broadcasts were typically limited to specific time slots during the day. CNN's continuous coverage allowed viewers to access news at any time, providing real-time updates on unfolding events worldwide.

CNN's success spurred the development of other 24-hour news channels globally. News organisations like BBC News and Sky News adopted the 24-hour news format in the following years. The proliferation of satellite and cable television played a significant role in making continuous news coverage feasible and accessible to a global audience.

Since then, the 24-hour news format has become a standard in the media landscape, with numerous news channels providing around-the-clock news coverage, events, and analysis. The advancement of the internet has further expanded the accessibility of news, enabling people to access updates anytime through online platforms.

Certainly, news stories can often be framed differently, emphasising either a "glass half empty" or a "glass half full" perspective. But more and more people are diving across the room for that remote control and turning over from the news. But why? Because most of the time, it's journalism based on being glass half empty. Here are some out-of-context examples that may sound familiar:

Public Health Crisis:

- Glass Half Empty: "Rising COVID-19 Cases Overwhelm Healthcare System."

- Glass Half Full: "Scientific Progress: Vaccines Show Promise in Combating the Pandemic."

Environmental Concerns:

- Glass Half Empty: "Climate Change Accelerates with Devastating Consequences."

- Glass Half Full: "Global Initiatives for a Greener Future Gain Momentum."

Education Challenges:

- Glass Half Empty: "Learning Loss Worsens as Pandemic Disrupts Education."

- Glass Half Full: "Innovative Approaches: How Schools Adapt to a Changing Educational Landscape."

Political Turmoil:

- Glass Half Empty: "General Election Creates Political Divisions, Threatening Social Stability."

- Glass Half Full: "Calls for Unity: Country Gets An Opportunity To Change Course."

It's essential to note that while there are extreme challenges, there are also positive aspects and progress occurring in modern society. Advances in technology, medical breakthroughs, social movements advocating for positive change, and increased awareness of social issues demonstrate that the glass isn't as empty as some people may think.

Optimism is not about denying reality or ignoring challenges; instead, it involves approaching life with a positive mindset and believing that, even in difficult situations, there is room for improvement and positive outcomes. It's a perspective that can influence how individuals cope with stress, make decisions, and navigate the complexities of life. So, is our news too 'glass half empty', making it harder for us to look at life through the lens of a glass that is half full?

Now, let's lightly touch on social media. Facebook, X, Instagram, and LinkedIn are all driven by algorithms, often showcasing curated and idealised versions of people's lives. This can trigger social comparison and feelings of inadequacy, contributing to pessimism. Additionally, the fear of missing out (FOMO) and the constant stream of information overload on these platforms can crank up our stress and negative emotions.

Confirmation bias plays a role as algorithms learn from user engagement. If users interact more with negative content, the algorithm prioritises and amplifies such information, deepening confirmation bias and pessimism. The lack of context in social media content further contributes to distorted perceptions of reality.

As social media users, are we aware of algorithmic influences that prevent us from having a more diverse perspective and limiting us when engaging with more balanced content? How familiar are you of this? But let's leave this here for now as we'll talk more deeply about social media later in the book.

Now, to touch on something very controversial. Are we as a society too zoomed in on being victims? Stay with me! "Victimhood culture" is often discussed in sociology and cultural studies to describe a social environment where individuals or groups emphasise their perceived victimisation to gain sympathy, support, or moral authority. This culture can manifest in various ways, influencing how people respond to challenges, conflicts, and social dynamics.

In a victimhood culture, those who present themselves as victims may claim moral authority based on their perceived suffering. This moral authority is used to shape narratives, influence opinions, and sometimes suppress dissenting views, making it harder to break the barrier of turning that challenge into triumph.

Now, here will be something you are most probably familiar with. Call-Out Culture, also known as cancel culture. Victimhood culture often involves a "call-out" or "cancel" dynamic, where individuals or groups publicly point out perceived wrongdoing or offensive behaviour. This can contribute to an environment where public shaming is used as a mechanism of social control. This is where we fail to agree to disagree and accept that other people's points of view may not always align with ours. Where would the world be if everyone thought, said, and did the same things?

In some cases, victimhood culture may lead to a hierarchy of victimisation, where different groups or individuals compete to be the most oppressed. Have you seen examples of this?

It's important to note that the concept of victimhood culture is a subject of debate, with some arguing that it brings attention to important issues of social justice, while others critique it for fostering an environment of hypersensitivity, moral grandstanding, and stifling open dialogue. Views on this concept can vary based on ideological, cultural, and individual perspectives.

A few years ago, I went to Washington D.C. Seeing the White House has always been on my bucket list - and I have heard nothing but good things about Washington D.C. I saw loads of fantastic stuff, stuff that I'll remember forever. But one of the things that stuck out in my mind is meeting a chap who called himself The Truth Conductor. He was holding a sign saying **'Stop Hating Each Other Because You Disagree With Each Other.'** This got me curious, so I went and had a chinwag with him. We discussed a range of things, mainly American politics. We disagreed on many things. But the one thing that was striking to me was that he could listen to other points of view without losing his shit. He was also highly optimistic about the future, and his spirit of hope was contagious. He said, 'Without hope, what do we have?' American politics is extremely toxic - but this dude has an infectious dose of hope that things will get better, life will get better, and hope and action will lead to that.

Picture of The Truth Conductor, sat outside
The White House in Washington D.C.

Now moving onto something slightly more personal to me. My Grandad Stan - one of the biggest characters the world has ever seen - and I was lucky enough to call him 'Grandad'. The poignant echo of his parting words — **"Keep Smiling"** — reverberates through the corridors of time for me. In these simple yet profound words lie timeless wisdom, a call to press on, no matter the circumstances. When life veers off its expected course, a smile becomes our shield and resilience, our sword. Let's unravel the layers of meaning concealed within the folds of a resilient spirit, drawing inspiration from those who, like my Grandfather, exemplified the art of keeping a positive outlook even in the face of adversity.

The dance between Glass Half Full and Glass Half Empty is the yin and yang of our existence. One complements the other, enriching the narrative of our lives. It's about finding the sweet spot between optimism and pragmatism, sipping from the cup of life with grace and resilience.

Perceptions of society's optimism or pessimism can be complex and nuanced, influenced by a combination of external factors and individual perspectives. Encouraging a balanced and informed view, promoting positive narratives, and emphasising collective efforts towards positive change can contribute to a more optimistic societal mindset.

So, dear reader, as you navigate the chapters of your own story, let the glass be not just an inanimate object but a metaphor for life's ever-shifting narrative. Whether you're sipping on the sweet nectar of positivity or acknowledging the bitter truths, relish the journey. Be the master mixologist of your own life, stirring in optimism, resilience, and a sprinkle of humour.

Let your mantra be to sip from the Glass Half Full in our day-to-day life. Remove those rose-tinted glasses of pessimism and negativity and start appreciating the nuanced melody of life in every drop. We have so much more to do as a world, as a society, as human beings - but we have so much to be grateful for. Sometimes, you feel like the odds are stacked against you. There will be times when you feel like practising your prison photo because life is testing you. But maybe, just maybe, we need to get over ourselves and think about the opportunities instead of being a victim; we need to wear the hat of optimism, not pessimism and see the glass half full rather than the glass half empty – and remember folks, **KEEP SMILING.**

Be Glass Half Full

FOOD FOR THOUGHT QUESTIONS ...

1) How often do you catch yourself dwelling on negative thoughts? What strategies can you employ to shift your focus towards a more positive mindset?

2) Think of a recent challenge. How might viewing it more optimistically change your approach and overall experience?

3) Reflect on a past failure. How did your perspective impact your ability to bounce back, and how could adopting a more optimistic attitude have altered the outcome?

CHAPTER 4
BE UNSOCIAL

"LIFE BEYOND THE FEED IS THE MOST A AUTHENTIC LIFE INDEED."

A harsh reality. The virtual tunes of social media often drown out the reality of life. This chapter invites you to step back from Kim Kardashian's backside, the keyboard warriors and the people with the rhythm of a corpse dancing to songs on Tik Tok. It invites you to think and dance to a different rhythm. It's not a call to abandon the digital dance floor entirely but to tango with intention, aware of the steps we take and the beats we follow.

First things first, let's open the pandora's box of social media and embark on a numerical journey through the digital landscape. Did you know that:

- On average, a person spends nearly 2 hours and 31 minutes per day on social media. Crunch the numbers, and that amounts to over 900 hours a year.

- Facebook has over 2.9 billion monthly active users - nearly nine times the population of the United States.

- 77% of businesses use social media to engage with their customers.

- 48% of us are turning to X, formally known as Twitter as our first news source.

- We share and send over 900 million emojis every day.

- Ronaldo and Messi are the most followed people on Instagram.

- TikTok is the most downloaded app ever.

These numbers stack up and paint a conclusion that we, as a modern society, are just too bloody social. Or are we? Stay with me.

Embarking on the digital journey of social media's evolution feels similar to unravelling the intricate layers of a technological onion. The early 2000s witnessed the emergence of digital trailblazers like FriendsReunited (ask your parents if you're in your 30s or younger) and MySpace, laying the groundwork for the seismic shift that was to come. Then, for the younger folk, choosing your top friends on Bebo and sharing your three loves a day with your secondary school crush became the latest craze. However, the arrival of Facebook in 2004 disrupted the status quo and rewrote the rules of global connectivity, heralding an era where virtual interactions became as significant as those in the physical world. Within this everchanging landscape, platforms like Bebo, once vibrant social landscapes, have now become a distant memory, now overshadowed by the towering giants of Instagram, Twitter, and Snapchat that dominate the contemporary digital realm.

I'm not here to claim I've mastered the art of avoiding social media or struck the perfect balance. I'll admit, I spend too much time scrolling, but I've been trying to Get Over Myself by making some small changes to break free from the social curse and spend more time on things that matter.

Years ago, me and a few of my mates visited one of the most authentic, exotic, and beautiful places on the European continent – yes, you guessed it. We went to Beindorm. We hit the Terra Mitica theme park, and here's the thing – despite having a blast, looking back at that day makes me cringe. Why?

Me and three of my mates decided to go on the log flume. Like absolute losers, we pre-planned a certain pose for our picture going down the steepest flume. I'll give you a clue about the pose: "You can have a good drink, you can have a good meal, you can do whatever you feel." Being the cool kids we are, we posed doing the YMCA, with me at the front doing the Y and my mates behind doing the M, C, and A.

We uploaded the pic on Facebook, and the likes poured in. Our ego's inflated like a hot air balloon, but when the attention plateaued at 99 likes, desperation kicked in. I even messaged people, begging for that extra like. It makes me cringe now, but back then; it was a big deal.

Looking back, it's a cringeworthy story that makes me realise how obsessed we were with social media validation. We were so caught up in the likes that we forgot to enjoy the moment on the log flume. Social media, for all its good, sometimes prevents us from being real, making us too self-centred and obsessed with our online image. Therefore, we really need to Get Over Ourselves.

In a world where feeds are carefully curated to showcase only the most dazzling moments, it's easy to forget that life is lived in unfiltered, unscripted bursts. For every breathtaking holiday photo, there exists a stack of laundry just out of the frame. This chapter beckons you to embrace the messiness of imperfection, as these are the brushstrokes that paint the masterpiece of authenticity.

Consider this eye-opening fact: over 80% of social media users experience anxiety when they can't access their accounts, prompting us to reflect on whether our virtual connections bring joy or silently generate stress. It's time to examine the toll of our digital dependencies. Personally, when I hit the gym, I often indulge in a sauna afterwards to ease any potential post-workout soreness. Yet, what consistently surprises me is witnessing individuals sitting in a sauna, heated to a cosy 95 degrees, glued to their phones. It serves as a stark reminder that, while not everyone, too many of us are tethered to our mobile phones – almost literally joint at the hip!

Our overreliance on digital communication could hinder our face-to-face interactions, leading to a potential decline in genuine, deep connections. There is more fake news, censoring and misinformation on social platforms than you can shake a stick at, contributing to us believing inaccurate or biased information. Excessive use and exposure to curated, tailored content that the algorithms have mastered for us may make us feel anxious, depressed or heavily comparing ourselves to others. Endless scrolling, notifications pinging, and constant connectivity can lead to distraction, taking a hammer to our productivity levels. There are also concerns over our data, and the potential misuse of personal information has become a significant issue. Is it just me, or have you ever thought about something - without googling it and then it appears as a sponsored ad on social media?

Understanding these impacts allows us to navigate social media mindfully, harnessing its benefits while mitigating potential adverse effects. Achieving a healthy balance and being aware of one's digital habits are essential for a positive relationship with social media. In essence, limiting social media is not entirely disconnecting but reclaiming control over how, when, and why we engage with these platforms. By doing so, individuals can break free from the pressures of the digital world, gain a clearer perspective on their lives, and focus on what truly matters to them.

Picture this: every ping, buzz, or chirp of your phone is a digital leash, pulling you away from the present moment. Did you know the average person checks their phone every 12 minutes? Now, imagine redirecting that attention to the people and the things around you. My friends, real connections flourish in the fertile soil of the present.

In 2020, when we battened down the hatches to shield ourselves from the COVID-19 pandemic, we started to see people dancing away to Jason Derulo's Savage Love song on a new platform called TikTok. TikTok has emerged as a transformative force, reshaping the social media landscape in so many ways. Its unique format, characterised by short-form videos set to music, has captivated a global audience and introduced novel dynamics to digital interaction.

First and foremost, TikTok revolutionised content creation by democratising the process. Unlike other platforms that often favour polished, curated content, TikTok thrives on authenticity and creativity. The algorithm driven "For You Page" on TikTok is pivotal in content discovery. By employing artificial intelligence to tailor content recommendations based on individual user preferences, TikTok creates an immersive and personalised user experience. This departure from chronological feeds has set a precedent, influencing other platforms like YouTube to reconsider their content delivery models by introducing YouTube #shorts.

TikTok's emphasis on virality and trend culture has significantly altered the dynamics of online fame. Overnight sensations and micro-celebrities can emerge from the platform, challenging the conventional route to stardom. The diversity of content, from dance challenges to educational snippets, contributes to a multifaceted user experience appealing to a wide demographic.

Moreover, TikTok has redefined the concept of collaboration. Duets and stitches enable users to seamlessly interact with and build upon each other's content, fostering a sense of community and interconnectedness. This collaborative spirit has set a trend within TikTok and influenced the other social giants.

The impact of TikTok on music and pop culture cannot be overlooked. The platform can catapult songs to viral stardom, influencing mainstream music charts and driving trends. Artists and brands have recognised the marketing potential, leading to strategic collaborations and promotional campaigns designed for the TikTok audience. Jason Derulo, Lizzo, and Celine Dion have all had songs that have done well because of the TikTok dances that people have created and boogied too, with their melodies in the background.

However, this transformative influence also raises ethical considerations. Issues like data privacy, content moderation, and the potential for exploitation or misinformation pose challenges that demand ongoing scrutiny. As TikTok continues to evolve and shape the social media landscape, it prompts a broader conversation about the responsibilities of platforms in navigating the intersection of creativity, entertainment, and user well-being.

As I've mentioned previously, everything in moderation, and social media is no outlier. But my frustration with social reached a new level in January 2023. On a crisp January morning, a mother of two, Nicola Bully, disappeared whilst walking her dog after dropping her kids at school in Lancashire. Social media, notably TikTok, took on an unexpected and troubling role. The story was unique – people don't just disappear off the face of the earth. As news of her vanishing spread, the platform became a digital arena where self-proclaimed "TikTok detectives" emerged, purportedly aiming to assist the investigation. However, the line between genuine concern and sensationalism blurred as individuals sought to exploit the tragic situation for personal gain through likes, views, and potential financial incentives.

The TikTok detectives, fueled by the pursuit of internet fame and the allure of viral content, started sharing unverified information, baseless speculations, and even engaging in online vigilantism. While possibly well-intentioned, their actions often had the detrimental effect of diverting attention and resources away from the official police investigation. In the relentless quest for attention and virtual validation, these TikTok users not only risked compromising the integrity of the case but also exploited a family's anguish for their own gain. Nicola's partner and her best friend were being accused of being involved in her death - by people who had never met or engaged with them. Absolutely shocking.

The tragedy of Nicola Bully's disappearance became a backdrop for a disturbing narrative where social media users, driven by the dopamine rush of likes and the prospect of internet stardom, blurred ethical boundaries. Exploiting a genuine tragedy for personal gain not only tarnishes the authenticity of online activism, which has seen some fantastic change over the years, but it raises profound questions about the impact of social media on serious criminal investigations. As we witness the convergence of social media and real-world tragedies, it prompts a critical examination of the responsibility that comes with the power of online platforms and the potential consequences of exploiting human suffering for digital acclaim.

Two weeks after she vanished, Nicola's lifeless body was sadly discovered in the river Wyre, close to where she went missing. You would like to think that in this horrific moment where one of our fellow citizens has been found dead, the wannabe inspector Clouseau's would put down their phones. But sadly, there were people there, armed with their phones, to try and capture the moment when her body was recovered from the river. Their moral compass was well and truly dropped.

Now you're probably thinking - well, that's a shameless minority of people doing this. And you are right. BUT ... these people produce this content because we, the public, watch it. When we watch it, other people watch it. When other people watch it, other people see it. That's how these things go viral. The harsh reality is that we are all responsible for this behaviour because we, as consumers, are adding fuel into the tanks of the morons who carry out this behaviour. The police investigation was most definitely impacted by the endless speculation, accusations and people flocking to the crime scene to get their five minutes of virtual fame. Maybe, just maybe, without the TikTok detectives, the police could have accelerated the investigation, and Nicola's friends and family could have had some closure much more quickly.

In today's digital playground, social media has transformed us all into everyday storytellers armed with nothing more than our trusty smartphones. We've become spontaneous reporters, capturing real-time events like aspiring news correspondents. This surge in citizen journalism is like a colourful mosaic of perspectives, offering a vibrant palette of voices often overlooked by the stodgy gatekeepers of traditional media. Fifty years ago, it would take hours, if not days, for any form of news to spread.

Now, it's just a matter of seconds. But like folk sometimes say, 'Don't believe everything you read in the papers', the same goes for social media - maybe on a much bigger scale. How much of what you see, read, or watch is genuinely authentic?

Let's now look at social media with a glass-half-full lens. Undoubtedly, social media has undeniably played a positive role in various aspects of our lives.

It facilitates instant communication, connecting people globally and fostering relationships. People can express themselves, share their achievements, and connect with like-minded individuals. It can provide support networks for people who need help, encouragement, or advice. It can inspire us, educate us and help us make decisions. It can raise awareness of the challenges facing society. And, of course, it can provide us with much-loved cat videos and dog pics. Families have been reunited, missing pets have been found, and relationships have formed - all through the power of social media! There is no doubt that social media has many positives and success stories.

Cast your minds back to 2014. The ALS Ice Bucket Challenge was a viral phenomenon that raised awareness and funds for Amyotrophic Lateral Sclerosis (ALS) research. Our timelines were filled with people sitting in their gardens throwing buckets of cold water over themselves and nominating their friends to do the same. Social media platforms catalysed this campaign, enabling people worldwide to share their participation and driving widespread engagement. The campaign eventually raised hundreds of millions of dollars for ALS research, helping to fund research into the fatal motor neurone disease - all whilst people were having fun and doing something that spread some much-needed positivity.

Social media platforms, including Facebook and Twitter,

have been instrumental in rapidly spreading information about missing people. Amber Alerts, for instance, are distributed through social media networks, reaching a broad audience extremely quickly. This immediate and widespread distribution has led to the safe recovery of missing individuals in numerous cases throughout the entire world!

The social gods are also powerful tools during natural disasters or crises. Platforms sometimes help facilitate relief efforts, connecting people with much-needed resources, and providing real-time updates. For instance, affected communities use social media to request help, share information, and organise assistance during hurricanes, earthquakes, or wildfires.

Then, there are Global Movements for Social Change. #MeToo, climate change and animal cruelty. Social media has accelerated global movements for social justice and change.

These examples illustrate the positive impact of social media in mobilising support, raising awareness, and facilitating collective action. While acknowledging these benefits, it's essential to recognise the responsibility that comes with the use of social media and the need for critical engagement to mitigate potential negative consequences.

As a modern society, we pretty much have access to piles of information at the drop of a hat. We've become so impatient. But along with becoming impatient, we've become fearful - and not in the sense that something terrible will happen to us. In a world teetering on the edge of digital excess, redefining FOMO – the Fear of Missing Out is imperative. We are crippled with fear that the party you saw your friend pose at was the wildest party of all time. Or you missed out on something remarkable in favour of recharging your social battery at home. What if, instead of chasing digital phantoms, we were missing out on the profound beauty of the present? Striving for balance becomes the antidote to the frantic pursuit of the virtual, allowing the real and the digital to coexist harmoniously. Please look at this in a glass-half-full view and think about JOMO - the Joy of Missing Out. JOMO is about embracing the liberation that comes with disconnecting – a day without the constant hum of notifications. During this day, you reclaim your life from the virtual noise and focus on you, your life, the nature around you, the family you love and all the other amazing things in your life.

Being social but unsocial is crucial for Getting Over Ourselves because it helps address several key factors that contribute to a healthier and more balanced life.

We can reduce the time and headspace used comparing ourselves to others. Through the screens on our phones, we see curated, idealised versions of people's lives. Essentially, they are the best parts of people's lives. Naturally, we compare and contrast our lives and often think, 'I want that', 'I wanna go there'. Turning down the dial on our virtual socialness can allow us to focus on our own journey without constantly comparing ourselves to others. Do we need to be constantly chasing the illusion of perfection? Or shall we embrace more of life's messy, imperfect, yet beautiful aspects?

Have you ever thought that an increasing amount of the global population is becoming more and more prone to mental and emotional health issues? Excessive use of social media has been linked to increased stress, anxiety, and feelings of inadequacy. Limiting exposure can help mitigate the negative impact on mental well-being and get us back in touch with putting our health first.

In many scenarios, I've met up with friends or family, only for both of us sometimes to sit there and be more engaged in some horrendous TikTok dance or life hack rather than catching up on life together. Real, meaningful relationships are built through genuine interactions. Not social ones. Putting down the phone when socialising can enable us to engage more deeply with those around us, fostering authentic connections and creating more meaningful memories.

Once you're done with this chapter, I dare you to go into your phone settings and look at your screen time. I'm sure it will surprise you. Most devices tell you the time spent on each app. We're all guilty of overindulging in the puddings of social media - but life to many people seems busier than ever. Have you ever said to yourself, 'I don't have time!' Or my personal favourite, 'There's not enough hours in the day'. We are all guilty of being busy doing nothing. But could your time spent on social media be better spent doing something more beneficial to you?

Time to look in the mirror, not your phone! Self-reflection is more vital than you'll ever know. How am I doing? What am I grateful for? What do I like about my life? What can I change for the better? Taming the social beasts provides the mental space necessary for introspection and personal growth. When was the last time you adequately reflected without being distracted by the endless messages and notifications?

Social media platforms are intentionally designed to be addictive, despite continuous denial from figures like Zuckerberg, Musk, and Gates. Getting hooked on these apps often leads to compulsive behaviour and excessive screen time, negatively impacting our sleep, mental health, posture and eyesight. It's crucial now more than ever to break free from this addictive cycle, shift our focus away from screens, and prioritize our well-being. To overcome this, we need to embrace a more un-social approach and rediscover the value of being present. You might wonder, 'Why is it more important now than ever?' My response is this... social media hasn't gone viral ... **YET!**

The future of social media is expected to involve several trends and developments shaped by technological advancements, changing user behaviours, and societal shifts. Here are some potential aspects that look to the future of social media.

Have you ever worn an augmented or virtual reality headset? Incorporating augmented reality (AR) and virtual reality (VR) technologies will likely enhance user experiences on social media, offering immersive interactions and new forms of content. The metaverse is being promised as this alternative life where you can enjoy a beer with friends without leaving the house. Is that the direction society will adopt? If so, count me out – it sounds shit!

Data sells. **Fact.** Years ago, I went onto a website to look at camper vans for a road trip around Scotland. My data was then sent to Facebook to hit me with camper van adverts - astonishing. With growing concerns about data privacy, there's an expectation for social media platforms to implement more robust privacy features, giving users greater control over their personal information. But they'll only go so far because our data is monetised.

In years to come, we'll continue to be Influenced by the Influencers. They will likely maintain their impact on marketing and content creation, evolving their strategies to stay relevant as platforms and audience preferences change. But ask yourself this: how many influencers influence us because they love a product or are passionate about something? On the flip side, how many of them are paid by companies to influence us because of their following?

Have you ever purchased something because it's been an

advertised on your timeline? Social commerce is expected to grow, with users being able to make purchases directly within social media platforms, blurring the lines between socialising and shopping.

Now, let's talk about Artificial Intelligence (AI), a concept Elon Musk has labelled as a potential threat to the world if it remains unregulated. AI is expected to play a larger role in content curation, recommendations, and interactions with chatbots. Personally, I've utilised ChatGPT to assist with work, find inspiration for my book, and even discover a spaghetti carbonara recipe. However, we're witnessing that AI has the capacity to generate things that never existed before, such as creating songs using artists' voices and generating images from other pictures, often presenting biased information. While AI holds promise in various essential areas like healthcare, it also has the potential to make social media more captivating, drawing us in. The question arises: as AI becomes more prevalent, how much of the content we encounter will remain truly authentic in the years to come?

As we stand on the edge of the unpredictable evolution of social media, I won't pretend to possess the clairvoyance of a mystic. The likelihood, however, is that it will continue to entwine itself more deeply in the fabric of our lives, responding to our needs, technological shifts, and societal dynamics. In this dance between the natural and the digital, new possibilities and challenges will undoubtedly emerge.

Returning to the essence of this chapter, my aim isn't to issue a digital exile or mandate the deletion of social media apps. I'm not here to dictate how you should live your life; that choice is entirely yours. Instead, I invite you to embark on a journey of introspection, challenging yourself to recalibrate your connection with both the digital and tangible realms. Is your balance intact, or do the scales of social interaction need a mindful readjustment? Consider the impact of social media on your well-being—does it uplift or undermine your sense of self?

For those engrossed in the captivating realms of social media, I propose a pause. Reflect on your digital footprint and ponder whether, just for a moment, do you need to turn down the volume of 'socialness.' Perhaps, in doing so, you can peel your eyes away from your screen and rediscover the vivid world unfolding right before you.

Life is a series of experiences meant to be lived authentically. In embracing a touch of 'unsocial' simplicity, we can liberate ourselves from the centre stage of self-centeredness, allowing genuine connections and meaningful interactions to reclaim their rightful place in the forefront of our social lives. Remember, life is for living after all!

Be Unsocial

FOOD FOR THOUGHT QUESTIONS ...

1) Evaluate your current relationship with social media. How has it impacted your real-life connections, and what changes can you make to strike a healthier balance?

2) When was your last day without any social media. How did it feel, and what insights did you gain about the role of technology in your life?

3) How can you set boundaries to prevent social media from becoming an addiction and reclaim more meaningful, in-person connections?

CHAPTER 5
BE DIFFERENTLY UNITED

STRENGTH LIES NOT ONLY IN STANDING FIRM
BUT IN THE COURAGE TO UNDERSTAND,
ACCEPT, AND EMBRACE THE BEAUTY OF
AGREEING TO DISAGREE

In the conversation of life, we're all nodding to the tune of sometimes not always seeing eye to eye with other people. Imagine it like the soundtrack of how we humans make our way through the world. We're jumping into the "It's ok to agree to disagree" zone, peeling back the layers of this lively but kind of messy mix. We're getting into the nitty-gritty, figuring out why having different points of view is like the secret ingredient in the crazy salad of our modern world.

In ancient Greece, notably in places like Athens, there was a vibrant intellectual and philosophical scene. Philosophers like Socrates, Plato, and Aristotle engaged in discussions and debates in public spaces known as agoras. These philosophers would often gather, along with other scholars and citizens, to exchange and challenge ideas.

The agora in ancient Greece was both a physical space and a symbol of open discourse. It was a marketplace where people not only traded goods but also exchanged thoughts and opinions. Philosophical discussions in the agora were crucial in shaping the intellectual landscape of the time, laying the groundwork for Western philosophy.

In today's digital age, social media platforms serve as vibrant spaces where diverse opinions come together in a dynamic exchange of ideas, promoting dialogue and thoughtful discourse. But it also causes division, hatred, and anger. 21st-century Britain is a canvas where passionate individuals pause traffic, aiming to raise awareness about environmental issues – which often is met with angry drivers shouting abuse whilst mounting the curb to get to work on time. There are picket lines of striking train drivers, nurses and posties seeking better pay. However, even though their efforts are supported by many, their endeavours are often met with chants of 'Lazy Bastards'.

Discussions often transform into vigorous debates within the spectrum of opinions on Covid vaccinations, lockdowns, Brexit, Donald Trump and other societal matters. The political landscape encompasses the Left, the Right, and the centre, where liberals, communists, socialists, nationalists, and globalists contribute their distinct perspectives.

As we navigate this diverse pot of ideas, a crucial question persists: **Amongst this mosaic of beliefs, who holds the torch of truth?** Alternatively, in our pursuit of understanding, have we momentarily overlooked the essential practice of agreeing to disagree, a cornerstone of harmonious coexistence with each other?

Understanding the difference between opinions and facts is like a maze. Opinions are like paintings made by people, adding their own colours to how they see things. Facts are like the strong bones that keep our discussions from becoming just a mix of different ideas. Knowing the difference between fact and opinion helps us handle disagreements better. Opinions can change because they're based on personal experiences, but facts are like a solid base we can all agree on—a stable point in our ever-changing thought process.

When people navigate disagreements with finesse, it's like orchestrating a musical exchange of ideas. Picture it as a skilled conductor guiding an orchestra – active listening takes the lead, allowing various opinions to harmonise the conversation. Thoughtful engagement is the supporting instrument, ensuring the discussion flows smoothly without hitting the wrong notes.

Disagreement is also a catalyst for growth and innovation. Rigorous debate can help refine, evolve and adapt ideas. The frictions of disagreement are the sparks that ignite the fires of progress. But what compliments disagreement like spaghetti compliments meatballs? It's Tolerance! Both disagreement and tolerance belong on the same plate. But more often than not - the tolerance is nowhere to be seen.

Have you ever witnessed or been part of a conversation morphing and escalating into an argument, with voices being raised using an aggressive twang? Or where disagreements might turn into personal attacks, where people's character is criticised rather than focusing on the issue at hand. How about someone refusing to listen to your point of view? Disregarding your ideas by withdrawing from a conversation or giving you the silent treatment altogether?

These behaviours are not constructive and often contribute to further discord. Effective communication and a willingness to understand differing perspectives are crucial for healthily resolving disagreements. Do you disagree? If so, that's cool - let's agree to disagree.

In 2018, I impulsively decided to embark on a journey to the mysterious and isolated land of North Korea. It's a place where life unfolds in stark contrast to the openness we enjoy in the Western world. While we can openly criticise our government without fear of severe repercussions, expressing dissent in North Korea could lead to doing a stint in the gulag. If you get caught trying to flee the country, it's not just the escapee that will face prison – it's their entire family. Even personal choices, like hairstyles are subject to limited legal options.

The experience of witnessing this stark difference in lifestyles left me with a mix of emotions. On one hand, there was fascination in exploring a way of life so different from our own. However, a prevailing sense of sadness lingered, realising the constraints faced by the people who live there.

Above all, the trip emphasised my gratitude for the liberties we cherish in our own country. The freedom to openly express dissent and celebrate the beauty of agreeing to disagree became even more apparent. It served as a poignant reminder of the value we place on individual expression and the diverse opinions that make up our society.

I feel blessed to live in a country where compromise is not a dirty word. Compromise is the process of finding a middle ground or a mutual agreement in situations where there are conflicting interests, opinions, or needs. It involves making concessions or adjustments to reach an acceptable solution. Now, you're probably going to think I've lost the plot, but whenever I think about compromise - I think about former Prime Minister Theresa May. Please stick with me!

"Never forget that compromise is not a dirty word. Life depends on compromise." The former prime minister bellowed these words on the steps of Downing Street whilst holding back the tears when she announced she was stepping down. Her words that day have left a lasting impression on me, and they frequently remind me that agreeing to disagree is one of the key ingredients to Getting Over Ourselves.

Crossing the ocean now to the United States. In July 2017, Senator John McCain made a significant move against his own party during the Senate vote on repealing the Affordable Care Act (ACA), often called Obamacare. Despite vocal criticism of the ACA, McCain surprised many by casting his vote against the Republican push to repeal portions of the healthcare law.

This decision to break ranks with his party and the subsequent "thumbs down" gesture symbolised his commitment to principles over personal bias. McCain, who had been diagnosed with brain cancer, emphasised the importance of regular order and collaboration in addressing healthcare reform. His vote was crucial in preventing the repeal effort from moving forward.

Whilst the ACA remains a subject of ongoing debate and discussion in America, McCain's willingness to go against his party demonstrated a commitment to principles, fostering a climate where differing views can coexist for the greater good. This moment reflected the idea that in politics, as in life, it's not only acceptable but sometimes necessary to agree to disagree for the sake of a more robust and inclusive democratic process.

From politics to football – or soccer if you're on the other side of the pond. Football is undeniably part and parcel of British culture. It's an integral and cherished aspect of daily life. From the roaring crowds in historic stadiums to the passionate cheers echoing through local pubs, football is more than just a sport in the United Kingdom; it's a communal experience that unites people across diverse backgrounds.

The passion for football is not confined to match days; it generates conversations at workplaces, social gatherings, and family dinners, becoming a shared language that goes beyond societal boundaries. The iconic football clubs, each with its storied history, are cultural landmarks that install a deep sense of pride and identity for fans. The rituals associated with football— whether it's the pre-match pint, the celebration of a goal, or the collective sigh of disappointment— they mirror the highs and lows of life itself.

However, football has witnessed negative trends like hooliganism and fights, which stain the beauty of the sport. Hooliganism involves rowdy behaviour by some fans, leading to violence, vandalism, and clashes with opposing supporters. These incidents not only jeopardise the safety of spectators but also tarnish the reputation of the game. Factors like rivalry, excessive alcohol consumption, and group dynamics contribute to some terrible behaviour. Football organisations and law enforcement agencies have implemented measures to curb hooliganism, including strict stadium regulations and increased security. It's safe to say that there are lots of things about football that creates division.

But it was on 18th April where my admiration for football fans reached new highs. News broadcasters started to break the news that a new European Super League had been announced. It was intended to be a breakaway league featuring some of the wealthiest and most successful football clubs in Europe. The idea was to create a closed competition with a fixed number of founding members, who would not face relegation, ensuring a consistent presence for these clubs in the league.

Twelve major football clubs from England, Spain, and Italy announced their plans to form the European Super League. The founding clubs included six from the English Premier League (Arsenal, Chelsea, Liverpool, Manchester City, Manchester United, and Tottenham Hotspur), three from La Liga in Spain

(Atlético Madrid, Barcelona, and Real Madrid), and three from Serie A in Italy (AC Milan, Inter Milan, and Juventus).

It's safe to say that there was backlash from the players, the managers, and the fans. Players were very critical of the plans - some publicly calling out the gatecrash of greed. Managers, who were not part of the decision-making process also expressed their views. At the time, Liverpool's colourful manager Jurgen Klopp said he 'hopes this Super League will never happen'.

But it was the fans who expressed the biggest backlash. Supporters of the founding clubs organised protests outside stadiums, condemning their clubs' involvement and expressing their dissatisfaction with the perceived betrayal of football's values. There were also calls to boycott the purchasing of club merchandise, season tickets, and tickets to games. Screens were being angrily tapped as fans were voicing their frustration on social media platforms - consistently bellowing their discontent to change the game they live and breathe. Anger and frustration were pointed towards the club owners for deciding to join the ESL without consulting the club, the management, or the fans. Even Boris Johnson weighed in on the argument, expressing he was ready to drop a "legislative bomb" on elite football clubs threatening to join the cartel breakaway Super League.

48 hours after the announcement, the British clubs withdrew from the ESL, thus eventually driving the ESL to an early grave. The announcement of the ESL served as a rare moment of unity among football fans, rising above traditional rivalries and differences. Whilst fans may passionately disagree within stadiums, pubs, and even on the pitch, the idea of football being sacrificed to the forces of greed was a source of collective disgust.

The prospect of a closed, elite league based on financial privilege rather than merit struck a chord. The spirit of competition, the unpredictable nature of the sport, and the principle that success should be earned on the pitch, not bought, prevailed. Fans, regardless of their allegiances, found themselves united in their rejection of the Super League, recognising it as a threat to the very essence of the game they love. The sense of solidarity among fans, as they rallied together to protect the integrity of the sport, showcased the profound impact that football has on communities.

I've never been big on football. But this series of events caught my eye because it was one of the most memorable and prominent times that I've seen people being differently united.

But not everything goes that way. In Northern Ireland, the Catholic vs. Protestant conflict, commonly known as the Northern Ireland conflict or The Troubles, has deep historical roots. Stemming from centuries of British rule in Ireland, religious and political divisions emerged. Catholics predominantly identify as Irish nationalists seeking independence, whilst Protestants align with unionists who wish to maintain ties with Britain. The late 20th century witnessed heightened violence, including bombings and shootings, carried out by paramilitary groups representing both communities. The Good Friday Agreement in 1998 brought a semblance of peace, but the legacy of The Troubles persists. The communities remain primarily segregated with children attending separate schools, and the sectarian divide influences political decisions.

The challenge of agreeing to disagree is entrenched in historical grievances and the fear of losing cultural identity. Despite progress, prejudices and mistrust endure, impacting social interactions and political negotiations. Individuals and families still grapple with the trauma of the conflict, and reconciling a divided society remains a formidable task.

In this transformative journey, identifying shared goals for peace is an opportunity to plant seeds of hope amidst the desolation. It is a collective recognition that despite the rubble, there are shared aspirations for a future free from the horrors of conflict.

Learning from history becomes a poignant exercise in understanding the human cost of physical conflict. It is an acknowledgement that each casualty, each destroyed home, and each shattered dream represents a profound human tragedy. The aspiration is not only to rebuild but to do so with a profound empathy that resonates with the grief and suffering endured. The hope, despite this devastation, is for a collective realisation that pursuing harmonious coexistence should be the world's biggest goal.

In wrapping up this chapter, let's champion the art of calm, rational, and respectful disagreement. Our world is a kaleidoscope of diverse perspectives, which adds depth and colour to our shared experiences. Not everyone will see things the same way, and that's perfectly fine. It's a reminder that each of us brings a unique set of experiences, beliefs, and viewpoints to the table.

When we encounter disagreements, let's approach them with an open mind. Do we need to ignite drama, or can we open our minds to the possibility of coexistence? The strength of our shared humanity lies in its diversity, and the key to peaceful coexistence is embracing this diversity, not despite it. The next time you find yourself at odds with someone, view it as an opportunity for growth, understanding, and building stronger connections. Through calm and rational conversation, we can close gaps, construct bridges, and nurture a positive atmosphere of coexistence.

In a world brimming with differences, let's celebrate them, let's appreciate them, and most importantly, let's learn from them. The willingness to agree to disagree forms the bedrock for a more compassionate and understanding world. As we move forward, let's carry the torch of respect, empathy, and the steadfast belief that even during disagreements, we can sing the lyrics of understanding, kindness, and unity.

FOOD FOR THOUGHT QUESTIONS ...

1) Reflect on a recent disagreement. How did you handle it, and what steps can you take to ensure productive conversations even when views differ?

2) Consider a situation where you changed your mind about a strongly held belief. What factors influenced this shift, and what did you learn from the experience?

3) How can you actively contribute to creating an environment where differing opinions are respected, fostering collaboration and understanding?

CHAPTER 6
GET OUT OF THE COMFORT ZONE

"COURAGE IS THE COMPASS THAT POINTS BEYOND COMFORT"

Picture this: a realm where everything is known, predictable, and safe. Sounds delightful. Comfort is the cosy armchair where we can all put our feet up and rest. It wraps around us like a warm blanket, shielding us from uncertainty.

Comfort, no doubt, has its merits. It's a sanctuary where stress is a rare visitor, and the daily grind takes hold of us. Familiarity brings a sense of control, like a captain navigating familiar seas.

Too much comfort and life becomes a routine where vibrancy, memories and growth begin to fade. Dreams become whispers drowned out by life's noise. But look outside the window, and you find life full of challenges and unknowns. It may seem daunting, but it's also where the colours to paint life's canvas await.

Imagine standing at the edge of your comfort zone, the border between the known and the unknown. Crossing that border might reveal the sweet smell of growth, resilience, and untapped potential. The discomfort of the unfamiliar is where innovation and self-discovery are found.

Yes, stepping into the unknown can be awkward, like a dance with two left feet. As you read this chapter, riddle me this: What lies beyond your comfort zone? What dreams are tethered to the edge of your familiar world, waiting to take flight?

So, my friend, let's embark on a quest beyond the cosy confines. Unravel the mysteries that lie beyond what you know; in doing so, you might discover a version of yourself that is more resilient, vibrant, and infinitely more captivating. After all, life's most profound stories are written outside the margins of the comfortable script.

Throughout human evolution, survival was a primary concern. Seeking comfort and avoiding discomfort were fundamental aspects of staying alive. Early humans who found secure, stable environments were more likely to prevent immediate threats, conserve energy, and survive to pass on their genes. Over time, this preference for comfort became ingrained in human behaviour.

Seeking comfort activates the brain's reward system, involving neurotransmitters like dopamine. When we experience comfort, pleasure, or familiarity, the brain releases dopamine, reinforcing the behaviour and creating a positive association with the comfort-inducing stimuli. This biological reward system motivates individuals to repeat behaviours that promote comfort.

Comfort is often associated with a lack of stress, and our brains naturally gravitate towards environments that reduce stress and give us an agro-free life. In today's complex world, comfort can take various forms – physical, emotional, or even intellectual. The brain has a stress response system designed to react to perceived threats. Seeking comfort is a way to mitigate stress. Comfortable environments or familiar situations trigger the brain to perceive safety, leading to a reduction in stress hormones like cortisol. This stress reduction reinforces the preference for comfort. Our pursuit of comfort aligns with the human desire for stability. Stable environments promote security, allowing individuals to focus on tasks other than immediate survival. This inclination toward comfort can be observed in daily routines, familiar spaces, and relationships.

Life can be bloody stressful at times, so reaching for our creature comforts is perfectly normal. But what is comfort? We, as humans, can feel both physically and emotionally comfortable. Let's start with our homes. Home is where the heart is. It's a place to relax, be ourselves, and feel secure. It's where the order and chaos happen. You can watch the TV in your pants, walk around naked, shoot the breeze, make wholesome meals, make love, organise your finances and shut out the world if you need to recharge your batteries. It gives us that physical and emotional comfort we very much need.

Or what about our routines? Daily routines and familiar surroundings include the same desk at work, walking the woofer around the same field, the same carriage on the train or even your favourite coffee from your local cafe. Being predictable makes us feel stable, which makes us comfortable.

For some people, it's clothing. We feel comfortable wearing those trusty pair of jeans or that cosy hoodie. For others, it could be heading to the mosque or living it up at church - being part of their community makes them feel wrapped up in that comfort blanket we're always reaching for. Then there are hobbies or activities. Whether it's reading a book, jazzing away on a musical instrument, or climbing a mountain - these hobbies create a comfortable and fulfilling experience for us.

All these creature comforts are a good thing! If we didn't

have regularity in our lives, we'd be all over the shop. Long-term stability can really help us. It keeps stress at bay, can make us more productive, provides emotional and mental stability, enhances our decision making and improves relationships. Imagine how hard it would be to keep a healthy relationship with someone if you're never in the same place for more than a few days. I've been blessed in the past to be able to travel for work. During some periods, I was travelling every single week. Living out of a suitcase on a set amount of clothes, possessions and toiletries can be mentally draining. I also had the privilege of backpacking with my mates around Asia and some other countries in my early twenties. I genuinely started to fear for my sanity - because I had no long-term stability. I would put something down and not remember where I put it - it left me thinking I was losing my marbles at a surprising rate. Me and my pals laugh at this now, but I once went into Macy's in New York to buy some gloves because it was cold enough to freeze the balls off a brass monkey outside.

These gloves were going to give me some sort of comfort. I paid twenty dollars for these lovely, thick, cosy gloves, only to leave the shop without knowing where the gloves were. I'd lost them within the space of the till and the exit. I felt like I needed to be sectioned. Losing stuff would rarely happen to me at home - I'm a bit of a freak, and everything always has its place, so I remember where everything is.

But of course, everything in life is always about balance. Every con has a pro, and every pro has a con - depending on how you view it. As I've mentioned in this book many times, everything in moderation! Too much comfort can be a bad thing. If we're too comfortable in life, it can lead us to stagnation. It's easy to become complacent and reluctant to try new things. If we're constantly wrapped up in our comfort blanket, we discourage ourselves from exploring new ideas, taking risks or being creative. If we don't leave our comfort zone, we don't learn as much as we could - and I'm not talking about academic learning; it could be a new park nearby that you never knew about or a new food you find tasty that you didn't think you would like. Not crossing the border from your comfort zone into whatever is available to you can be isolating - you end up relying too much on your comfortable armchair, which can lead to all manner of things like depression, no sense of self-worth, and low self-esteem. Opportunities are plenty if you want opportunity. A reluctance to embrace discomfort may lead to missing that opportunity that might be a game changer - whether it be an opportunity to earn money, advance your career, get fitter or feel better after an illness. The more opportunities we embrace, the more resilient we become.

Then there is the physical side. At the age of 30, my Mum still seems to think I still eat nothing but chicken nuggets and chips. I often say to her, 'Mum, I have tried different foods since I moved out, you know'. 80% of my life, I've not looked after myself - I stayed within my comfort zone regarding my physical body. I love burgers, hot dogs, and Nando's - I'm a vegan's worst nightmare. I'm not a big fan of discussing health and fitness with others because, trust me - I'm no David Beckham. But staying within your comfort zone when it comes to food and your body can lead to an avenue of different issues.

Move it or lose it - a mantra that reminds us that our bodies are on this earth to be used, and we need to put the right fuel in us to keep the wheels turning. We all know some idiot who's put petrol in a diesel car at some point (if it's you, you're an idiot). Putting the wrong fuel in our bodies won't give us what we need to get going. If you leave your car on the drive for months without using it, the battery probably dies, it gets dirty, or it takes a while to start. Our bodies are not that different to cars. Various components of our bodies work together to propel us in the right direction.

Personal growth and transformative experiences happen at the coordinates beyond your comfort zone. It's a realm where you discover capabilities you never knew existed and confront challenges that propel you forward. The discomfort of the unfamiliar is the catalyst for innovation and resilience, fostering adaptability in the face of life's uncertainties. Beyond the safety net of the familiar lies a landscape of opportunities waiting to be seized. Embracing discomfort is not merely a departure from the routine; it's a voyage into self-discovery and empowerment. It's about pushing boundaries, overcoming fears, and realising the profound truth that the magic of life often unfolds at the edges of our comfort zones. In these uncharted territories, you forge a more resilient and resourceful version of yourself, capable of navigating the ever-changing currents of the human experience.

After lockdown, I noticed I'd put on a bit of timber. I decided to buy some scales to see the damage - thinking worst case scenario I put on a stone, taking me to around the 16 stone mark. I ripped open the scales, tossed the instructions written in Chinese to one side and stepped on. I saw 18 stone 4lbs. I thought, 'What a load of cheap Chinese shit these scales are'! Until it sunk in, I looked in the mirror, with my double chin staring back at me, and I had that moment of realisation that it was time to grab the passport - because I needed to cross the border and leave my comfort zone.

All my life, I've been a proper gym dodger - it's full of meathead bodybuilders who look scary and take selfies in the mirror.

My next-door neighbour is a Personal Trainer; he got me used to a gym environment. He holds the mirror up to me when I leave my comfort zone but calls me out when I return to the safety of my comfort blanket. Over the last year, I've made some fantastic progress fitness-wise - I've gone from chins to chin, and it's opened my eyes to how important it is to look after ourselves. I'm still not the biggest gym fan, but I always remind myself that each time I walk down that staircase after a workout at my local gym, I've made progress and left my comfort zone. It's such a great feeling. Working out with a personal trainer who is as fit as a butcher's dog can sometimes be frustrating - there have been times when he's doing pull-ups with ease, and I'm doing a pull-up looking like I'm constipated. But that has taught me one important thing. Everyone's comfort zone starts from a different place. To some people, leaving their comfort zone is to do 20 pull-ups. To some people, it's to do a pull-up. To some people, leaving their comfort zone is to do a marathon. To some people, it's walking a few steps. To some people, it's moving house. To others, it can be leaving the house. But the fantastic thing about the comfort zone border is that it never stays in the same place. Each time you leave the vicinity, it will be pushed ever so slightly in front of you - keeping up with your progress.

Let's dive into one of the top moments on British TV – and no, I'm not referring to the 'David's Dead' incident. That was the time in the celebrity Big Brother house when everyone thought David, a contestant, had passed away. It turns out they confused David Gest with the iconic David Bowie's unfortunate passing.

I'm talking about a moment of TV gold where Musharaf Asghar, who appeared in the television documentary series "Educating Yorkshire" on Channel 4, threw himself out of his comfort zone in the best way possible. In the series, Musharaf was a student at Thornhill Community Academy in West Yorkshire, England. He struggled with a severe stutter, which massively affected his confidence and communication skills, making him frustrated and isolated. He found it challenging to express himself verbally, impacting his ability to participate fully in classroom activities.

Despite the challenges, Musharaf genuinely desired to overcome his stutter and improve his communication skills. This willingness to confront his difficulties showcased his resilience and determination. He was all packed to get the next plane out of his comfort zone to overcome something holding him back.

Musharaf's English teacher, Mr. Burton, used a unique and unconventional method to help him overcome his stutter. Inspired by the movie "The King's Speech," Mr. Burton encouraged Musharaf to use headphones and listen to music while speaking. The idea was that the music would help him overcome the mental blocks associated with his stutter.

Clutching a bit of paper, with only Musharaf and Mr Barton in the room, Musharaf started to read. To their surprise, he was pushing out his words, loud and clear to his teacher. With Mr. Burton's support and guidance, Musharaf made significant progress in speaking more fluently. This then led Musharaf to give a speech to his peers in an assembly hall. He stood at the front of your typical school hall, curtains whooshing in the background, with all eyes on him - Musharaf was reading from the piece of paper in front of him - he finally had a voice! Teenage lads who would usually give it the Billy big Bollocks in the playground we're crying in the assembly hall. This heart-warming and inspiring moment captured the attention of the country, and no doubt inspired many people with speech impediments.

The episode resonated with viewers because it portrayed a

genuine and heartfelt journey of overcoming adversity and leaving your comfort zone. Musharaf's story symbolised resilience, the power of unconventional teaching methods, and the importance of empathy and support. It also highlighted the transformative role that teachers can play in our lives, going beyond traditional approaches to address individual needs. The positive outcome of Musharaf's journey outside the comfort zone opened many doors for him - he's now a Public Speaker. This a fine example of how he left his comfort zone, battling resilience, grabbing the keys to opportunity and overcoming the obstacles in his way.

But would Musharaf have stepped outside his comfort zone if Mr Barton didn't push him to? The answer is we don't know. But Mr Barton here is the silent saint. People change people. That's not to say that everyone you meet will change your life, but the people around you can help you - giving you that comfort while pushing you out of your comfort zone. Think of it like a shot in the arm. By strategically incorporating small doses of comfort into leaving one's comfort zone, individuals can navigate the transition more smoothly, ultimately pushing our personal growth and development.

A small, manageable step towards your North Star provides a sense of accomplishment without overwhelming discomfort. This incremental progress builds confidence and can encourage individuals to take further, more significant steps outside their comfort zones. Progress trumps perfection, and as I said before, the border of your comfort zone always moves with you.

Having someone help you or being able to confide in can serve as a psychological safety net. It reassures individuals that they'll be able to speak to someone about their progress, bounce ideas around and get stuff off their chest if they face a setback.

That small dose of comfort whilst working towards your goals can shift one's mindset from a fixed mindset to a growth mindset. By framing discomfort as an opportunity for learning and growth, individuals become more open to challenging themselves.

It's about balancing the scales of comfort and discomfort. If you were to drop yourself into the Amazon rainforest right now, as you currently are, you wouldn't survive. You might stand a chance if you were dropped into the Amazon rainforest with a map, a compass, warm clothes, a sleeping bag, and some other comforts.

But many things draw us back from crossing that border from the comfort zone to the unknown. The fear of not succeeding or making mistakes can be paralysing, preventing us from taking risks and trying new things. The unknown can be unsettling, and many prefer the predictability of familiar situations. The uncertainty of what lies outside the comfort zone can be a significant deterrent. Many of us lack self-confidence, limiting our belief that we can successfully handle challenges or navigate unfamiliar territory. We are also concerned about how others perceive us, which can be a powerful deterrent. The fear of judgment or criticism from peers and society can discourage people from deviating from the norm. Previous negative experiences or trauma can instil the fear that history will repeat itself, leading to avoidance of anything that triggers similar emotions. Then there is the idea of perfectionism. A desire for perfection can lead to a fear of making mistakes. People may avoid situations where they are not guaranteed success or flawless performance. But is perfection real? Is it an illusion? We'll talk more about this later in the book.

Understanding these excuses and working to address them

can empower individuals to overcome the obstacles holding them back from leaving their comfort zones. Now you're probably thinking, did I read that right? You bet your bottom dollar I did - they are EXCUSES. Stay with me.

Excuses are rationalisations or justifications we make to avoid taking responsibility for our actions, behaviours, or decisions. They often serve as a way to explain why we have yet to achieve a particular goal, fulfil a commitment, or take necessary action. Recognising and overcoming excuses involves a combination of self-awareness, accountability, and a proactive mindset.

What is the recipe for an excuse?

- **350g of Avoidance of Responsibility:**

Excuses shifts blame away from ourselves and onto external factors, circumstances, or other people.

- **2 Tablespoons of Repetition:**

Excuses can become habitual, creating patterns that hinder personal growth and progress.

- **A dusting of Fear of Failure:**

Excuses may arise from a fear of facing failure or judgment, providing a protective shield for the ego.

So, how do we recognise our excuses? Holding up our mirror and understanding the reflection is a powerful way of recognising our excuses. Regular self-reflection helps identify patterns of behaviour. What goal have you not met that you wanted to meet, and why? We are all guilty of saying, 'I can't', 'it's too difficult', or my personal favourite, 'I don't have time. When you say this, do you mean it? What do you want to do but need more time for? Is there anything you can sacrifice or adjust in your life right now to make the time? If you consistently attribute not leaving the comfort zone because of challenges to external factors - it's most likely an excuse.

Recognising and overcoming excuses is an ongoing process requiring self-awareness and personal development commitment. By taking ownership of our actions, can we break free from the cycle of excuses and move toward a more empowered and fulfilling life?

This is where we need to Get Over Ourselves. By accepting responsibility for our actions and decisions, we can acknowledge that we have control over our responses to situations. Have you been meaning to go for that run? Have you been meaning to jump on the scales? You are the only person in the way of that, so Get Over Yourself . How valid are your excuses? Are they based on facts or driven by fear or self-doubt? My old Headteacher, Mr Kibble, once told me in the corridors of my English block at school - Fail to prepare, prepare to fail. Having a plan is always an excellent way to make progress in small, manageable chunks. Share that goal with someone you trust, get a mentor, and make yourself accountable. Does your mindset need to shift from dwelling on problems towards finding solutions? If your gates to growth are closed, blow those bad boys wide open.

If we get over ourselves and get out of our comfort zone - we will embrace change, become resilient, innovate, solve problems, learn new things and thrive.

My friends, life is a magnificent adventure, a journey filled with opportunities waiting to be seized. We, as humans, are not designed to linger perpetually in the cosy cocoon of our comfort zones. Rather, life's vibrancy lies in the kaleidoscope of experiences that unfold when we venture beyond the familiar. Picture it as a grand banquet; the tastiest dishes are not found within the confines of routine but in the uncharted territories of challenge and discovery.

Life's brevity is not a constraint but a call to action. In life's theatre, the spotlight beckons us to dance with uncertainty, to take the stage and revel in the joy of overcoming. So, let's infuse our days with the spirit of adventure; let's be the architects of our own stories, the maestros of our symphony. Embrace the challenges with a playful heart, for it is through daring leaps that we paint the most vibrant strokes on the canvas of our lives.

Get Out The Comfort Zone

FOOD FOR THOUGHT QUESTIONS ...

1) Identify a recent situation where you stepped out of your comfort zone. What did you learn from the experience, and how did it contribute to your personal growth?

2) Consider an area of your life where you've become too comfortable. What small changes can you make to introduce healthy challenges and stimulate progress?

3) How can you encourage others around you to embrace discomfort as a catalyst for growth and innovation?

CHAPTER 7
CONTROL THE COMPARISON

"FOCUS ON YOURSELF. DON'T GET LOST IN OTHER PEOPLE."

L et's rewind to the 90s when the internet was a new born, and the sound of dial-up connections echoed through households. We embarked on a journey of peculiar crazes that would shape the landscape of many childhoods. Let's take a stroll down Nostalgia Lane.

First of all, there were the discs of destiny. Also known as Pogs. Those colourful cardboard discs embellished with whimsical designs, ruled the playgrounds with an iron fist. Gathering in huddles, kids would engage in epic Pog battles, fervently slamming their heavy metal or plastic slammers onto stacks of Pogs, hoping for a triumphant victory. The clinking sound of Pogs colliding echoed in school playgrounds, creating a culture of childhood competition.

Then, everyone became masters of the string as we entered the yoyo era. In the world of Yoyos, every kid aspired to be a maestro of tricks. From the basic "Walk the Dog" to the elusive "Around the World," Yoyos were the portable stage for a mesmerising performance. The rhythmic clicking of the Yoyo's ascent and descent became a soundtrack for countless afternoons perfecting gravity-defying stunts.

Enter the realm of Beanie Babies, where plush creatures became prized possessions. Kids became amateur collectors, carefully curating their Beanie Baby crew, convinced that these cuddly companions would one day be worth a fortune. The hunger for limited editions and rare finds turned playdates into trading sessions and bedrooms into miniature Beanie Baby museums.

Soon after the beanie baby era, we entered the reign of scented scribbles. A peculiar phenomenon wafted through the air in the classroom – the fragrance of smelly pens. These writing instruments decorated notebooks with vibrant ink, leaving a trail of delightful scents in their wake. Each pen stroke was a sensory adventure from watermelon to bubble gum, transforming mundane notetaking into a fragrant escapade.

No discussion of '90s crazes is complete without the mention of Pokémon cards. Decks of these colourful cards featuring Pikachu, Charizard, and many pocket monsters became coveted treasures. Playground alliances were forged through strategic trades, and the thrill of uncovering a holographic card was a triumph that resonated through the halls of schools worldwide.

Now you're probably thinking, what has this got to do with us humans being devotees to comparison. Well, it was drilled into us from an early age. If you can relate to any crazes I spoke about, I want you to cast your mind back. Did you want a Yoyo, a beanie baby, a smelly pen or a specific Pokémon card simply because someone else had one? The answer is most probably a big fat yes!

From the sandbox to the classroom, our upbringing intricately weaves comparison threads into the fabric of our early experiences. With school grading structures and competitive environments, educational systems mould children into habitual comparers from a young age. Well-meaning parents, aiming to motivate, might unintentionally encourage comparisons among siblings or friends, setting the stage for a lifetime of measuring up. Traditional and social media bombard children with images and narratives that often set unrealistic standards, contributing to the early seeds of comparison. Peer interactions become a training ground for this habit as children observe and compare themselves to friends, whether in possessions, achievements, or abilities.

Reward systems in schools and extracurricular activities inadvertently fuel the comparison fire by consistently highlighting and rewarding specific achievements. Cultural expectations and societal norms further shape children's perceptions of success and failure, anchoring the comparison mindset in conventional markers of worth. In this cauldron of childhood experiences, the roots of comparison take hold, laying the foundation for a lifelong dance with measuring up. Recognising these influences becomes paramount in breaking free from the comparison trap, allowing the promotion of a more self-affirming and authentic sense of identity.

The inclination of humans to compare themselves to others is deeply rooted in our evolutionary history and societal dynamics. Returning to our ancestors' quest for survival, comparison was a fundamental instinct to ensure access to essential resources. As we navigate the intricate web of social interactions, comparing ourselves becomes intertwined with our search for validation and identity, shaped by societal norms and expectations placed upon us since childhood. This comparison habit often functions as a benchmark for progress, motivating us to set goals and achieve more. The emotional rollercoaster that accompanies comparison is orchestrated by our brains, releasing feel-good chemicals when we perceive ourselves doing better and causing feelings of inadequacy when we fall short. Cultural influences and the desire for improvement also significantly fuel this comparative instinct. Essentially, the impulse to compare is a complex interplay of survival instincts, societal conditioning, emotional responses, and a genuine quest for personal growth. Recognising these roots can be crucial to breaking free from the comparison trap and embracing a more authentic, individual path.

The science behind comparing ourselves to others delves into the intricate workings of psychology and neurobiology. Our brains, finely tuned by evolution, are wired to engage in social comparison, a phenomenon with roots in the release of neurotransmitters. When we perceive ourselves as surpassing others, our brains reward us with a surge of dopamine linked to pleasure and reinforcement. Functional magnetic resonance imaging (FMRI) studies have pinpointed specific brain regions central to this process, including the prefrontal cortex, amygdala, and ventral striatum, each playing distinct roles in decision-making, emotional responses, and reward processing. Social psychologist Leon Festinger's Social Comparison Theory further emphasises the influence of comparison on self-perception and self-esteem, tracing it back to our evolutionary past as a survival strategy within social groups. Mirror neurons, the cognitive mirroring of observed actions, and ongoing cognitive evaluations contribute to this comparison festival. Recognising the scientific underpinnings of this behaviour provides valuable insights into our inherent inclination to measure ourselves against others. It underscores the importance of cultivating self-awareness in navigating the complexities of social comparison.

The Social Comparison Theory, introduced by Festinger in 1954, remains one of the foundational theories exploring why individuals engage in social comparison. This theory asserts that people determine their social and personal worth by evaluating their abilities and opinions compared to others. The comparison process serves as a mechanism for self-evaluation and helps individuals assess their abilities, opinions, and beliefs.

Festinger's Social Comparison Theory further distinguishes between two types of social comparison:

Upward Social Comparison:
In upward social comparison, individuals compare themselves to others who are perceived as superior or more successful. This type of comparison may motivate individuals to improve themselves and strive for higher achievements.

Downward Social Comparison:
Downward social comparison involves comparing oneself to others who are perceived as less successful or inferior. This type of comparison can enhance one's self-esteem by emphasising one's strengths and positive attributes.

The Social Identity Theory, proposed by Henri Tajfel and John Turner in the 1970s, explores how people categorise themselves and others into social groups. Social comparison plays a role in this theory as individuals seek to enhance their self-esteem by positively differentiating their own group from others.

Even though its nature and impact have evolved over time, the UK still has a social class system. The UK's social class structure has traditionally been influenced by factors such as occupation, education, income, and family background. The traditional class divisions include upper class, upper-middle class, middle class, working class, and lower class. However, it's important to note that societal structures and classifications are complex and can change. Over recent decades, there have been discussions about the blurring of traditional class boundaries and the emergence of a more diverse and fluid social landscape. Nearly all societies have some form of social stratification.

In the mix of Indian culture, especially in Hindu traditions, a notable social hierarchy exists. This system classifies individuals into distinct social groups or castes, each traditionally linked to specific occupations and social roles. Despite ongoing efforts to address the inequalities stemming from the caste system, its impact remains evident in various facets of Indian society. In the context of Hindu culture in India, there are four primary castes.

1. **Brahmins (Priests and Scholars):** Traditionally considered the highest caste, Brahmins were associated with priestly duties, teaching, and scholarship.

2. **Kshatriyas (Warriors and Administrators):** This caste included warriors, rulers, and administrators. Their responsibilities were to protect the land and maintain law and order.

3. **Vaishyas (Merchants and Landowners):** Vaishyas were involved in agriculture, trade, and commerce. They played a crucial role in economic activities.

4. **Shudras (Labourers and Service Providers):** Shudras were traditionally engaged in manual labour and service-oriented professions. They served the other three groups.

It's important to note that the caste system has been a subject of criticism due to the social inequalities and discrimination it has perpetuated. Modern India has made significant strides to promote social justice, equality, and inclusivity, and various laws and policies have been implemented to address historical injustices associated with the caste system. However, challenges and disparities still exist and it's not just India with a social hierarchy. Throughout history, many countries have had a prominent social class system. This hierarchical structure naturally leads to comparisons between individuals and groups. But looking at this from both sides of the coin, is it a good thing to motivate and inspire? Or a bad thing due to inequality and injustice?

Even the film Mean Girls is a fantastic representation of different social groups that can form in a school setting. For those who have not seen the film, Mean Girls is a movie from 2004. It's all about Cady, played by Lindsay Lohan, trying to survive high school. She starts dealing with this crazy social jungle and ends up tangled with the popular girl group "The Plastics," led by a girl named Regina George. There's drama, backstabbing, and a few laughs as Cady learns the ropes of high school life. It's a hilarious take on the ups and downs of teenage social scenes. In the film, you have the following social groups:

- **The Plastics:** The popular girls led by Regina George. They are fashionable, socially dominant, and set the trends in the school.

- **The Mathletes:** The academically inclined students who participate in math competitions.

- **The Burnouts:** Often associated with smoking and laid-back attitudes, they are portrayed as a more alternative or rebellious group.

- **The Cool Asians:** A group of students from Asian backgrounds who are stereotypically seen as cool and trendy.

- **The Art Freaks:** Students with a passion for the arts. They are shown creating visually striking and unconventional art.

- **Unfriendly Black Hotties:** A term used to describe an exclusive clique of African American girls.

- **Varsity Jocks:** The athletic and sporty students who are part of various sports teams.

Cady starts by observing and analysing different social

groups in her high school. As she navigates the complex social hierarchy, she tries to fit in "The Plastics." This involves adapting her behaviour, style, and values to align with theirs. Throughout the movie, Cady's experiences reflect the broader theme of how teenagers often compare themselves to various social groups in their quest for acceptance and belonging. Eventually, Cady rejects the Plastics when she realises the negative impact of conforming to their toxic behaviour. After gaining insight into the consequences of betraying her true friends and embracing superficiality, she decides to break away from the Plastics. Cady's rejection signifies her personal growth and the rejection of a shallow and harmful social structure. It also emphasises the movie's message about the importance of authenticity and genuine connections over superficial popularity. Cady eventually becomes friends with Janis and Damian, who are initially outsiders in the high school social scene. Janis and Damian provide Cady with genuine friendship and support, contrasting with her superficial relationships with the Plastics. Through her friendship with Janis and Damian, Cady learns valuable lessons about authenticity and the importance of genuine connections. It's an interesting example, but this film shows that it's easy to lose your way if you compare yourself and conform with the wrong people. It highlights the importance of keeping it real, being true to yourself and not succumbing to the social pressures surrounding us.

If you were to ask your Alexa: What is addiction? She would say something along the lines of it being a chronic condition characterised by compulsive engagement in a substance or behaviour despite adverse consequences, stemming from changes in the brain's structure and function. It involves a loss of control, persistent cravings, and continued use despite the negative impact on one's health, relationships, or daily life. Let's call a spade a spade, there are many people throughout the world that are addicted to social media. When we talk about addiction, we often think about alcohol, drugs and gambling. People attend meetings like alcoholics anonymous where they discuss their feelings, cravings, setbacks as well as their successes. Do we need to start setting up social media anonymous groups?

The rise of social media and our addiction to it has significantly contributed to the increase in social comparison frequency and intensity for several reasons. Social media platforms encourage users to share curated snapshots of their lives. People often present the highlights, achievements, and positive aspects of their experiences, creating a skewed and idealised version of reality. Constant exposure to these curated posts can lead to unrealistic comparisons with others' seemingly perfect lives. Users tend to showcase their best moments, creating a "highlight reel" of their carefully curated lives. This constant exposure to others' successes and joyful moments can lead to a distorted perception that everyone else is thriving, exacerbating feelings of inadequacy in comparison.

A few years ago, I made the decision to step off the Instagram train. One evening, while alone at home, I found myself scrolling through Instagram, feeling a growing sense of jealousy and envy. At that moment, it seemed as though everyone else had a more exciting life than mine. Despite having travelled the world, enjoying the company of the best family and friends, maintaining a vibrant social life, and having a fulfilling job, it still didn't feel sufficient.

I came to the realisation that I was measuring my fantastic life against the curated highlight reel of someone else's experiences. This comparison made me feel ungrateful for the abundance of amazing things in my life. So, in a moment of clarity, I took a decisive step – I pressed and held my finger on the Instagram icon and ultimately chose to delete the app. Personally, it turned out to be the best decision I've ever made. It freed me from the addictive cycle of constantly comparing myself to others.

Likes, comments, and shares on social media often serve as a form of social currency. The pursuit of social validation can lead individuals to compare the popularity of their posts and the number of followers with those of others, impacting self-esteem and self-worth. We've all been there, watching the likes roll in on a post, constantly topping up your dopamine levels. I often look at people's snaps on social media and think, 'their skin looks great' or 'they look really tanned'. The reality is their picture is probably plastered with filters.

In 2021, the University of London's Gender and Sexualities Research Centre unveiled a report that states that 90% of young women reported using filters or editing their photos. They used this to reshape their nose, appear to weigh less, and have whiter teeth. The prevalence of carefully edited images on social media contributes to unrealistic beauty standards. Continuous exposure to flawless images can lead to body dissatisfaction and low self-esteem as individuals compare themselves to digitally altered representations.

It's time for one of those hands-up moments. The other day, I watched an ex-love islander make a gourmet meal of Chicken Dippers, potato waffles and smiley faces on YouTube. About 60 seconds in, I said to myself, 'What the fuck are you doing, Jack?!' In recent years, we've witnessed the meteoric rise of influencer culture, a phenomenon where individuals, often with a significant social media following, wield considerable influence over their audience. This cultural shift has reshaped how we consume information, make purchasing decisions, and even define societal trends. Let's delve into the factors contributing to the rise of influencer culture and why humans are increasingly turning to influencers. They often portray aspirational lifestyles that captivate their audience. Whether it's luxurious travel, stylish fashion, or glamorous events, followers are drawn to the possibility of emulating these lifestyles. The aspirational aspect creates a desire for the products and experiences influencers showcase. Influencers provide a sense of human connection as our lives become more digital. Their stories, interactions, and engagement with followers bridge the gap between the virtual and real worlds, offering a facade of companionship in the digital age. However, influencer culture has always been around. It's not something new. Princess Diana, Joan Collins and David Bowie had a massive influence on people's fashion in the 1980s - we just consumed the content differently in the format of magazines, newspapers and television.

I want to touch on a lady called Belle Gibson. In early 2013, a young Australian lady called Belle graces the screens of Instagram revealing to the world she unfortunately had terminal brain cancer and was given four months to live. After a few months of chemotherapy treatment, Belle revealed that she stopped her treatments and went down the route of alternative treatments and healthy eating. She posted on a regular basis that healthy whole foods and different therapies were in fact helping, curing her inoperable brain tumour. She gave hope to thousands of people suffering from cancer. She brought light to those facing darkness.

Belle attracted a humungous following on her social media accounts. It's a story that engrossed thousands of people. She went on to create The Whole Pantry App, offering followers the chance to pay for access to recipes and advice from this self-proclaimed health expert. She also published a book - packed with cancer curing wholesome recipes. Her success resulted in substantial financial gain and she pledged to donate a portion of her earnings to various charitable organisations and she even worked with families whose children were suffering from terminal illness.

Two years after gaining fame on Instagram, Belle seemed to be defying the odds, appearing alive, healthy, and vibrant. To her followers, she was defying the odds of terminal cancer and had managed to fight it off. To the masses, Belle was curing terminal cancer by drinking coconut water smoothies. However, in March 2015, everything took a dark and dramatic turn. Both the media and those around her began to cast doubt on the authenticity of her story and Belle's bubble was about to be well and truly burst. The police initiated an investigation and eventually, Belle admitted to fabricating the entire narrative. When questioned by The Australian Women's Weekly about the veracity of her cancer story, she confessed, stating, "No. None of its true."

Belle had shockingly led everyone down the garden path of believing there was hope. This despicable behaviour led genuine sufferers to withdraw from treatment in favour of Belle's approach. This serves as a crucial reminder that we must be alert, aware and mindful of the content influencers push onto our screens.

Influencers display idealised lives, fostering unrealistic standards that make followers compare and feel dissatisfied with their lives. It contributes to our feeling of materialism and a constant desire for consumer goods, which can financially strain us. Unrealistic expectations set by influencer portrayals may lead to dissatisfaction with partners, friends, or family members who don't meet these idealised standards. In fashion, fitness, and beauty, influencers may fuel body image concerns, pressuring individuals to conform to specific beauty ideals and affecting self-esteem. Younger audiences may be vulnerable to the influence of influencers. Exposure to unrealistic standards at a young age can shape their perceptions of normalcy and impact their self-esteem as they grow older. While influencers can be positive role models and sources of inspiration, individuals need to approach their content critically and maintain a balanced perspective - essentially, do we need to be influenced as much as we are and are we being influenced by the right type of people?

Whatever way you look at it, comparison is part of our daily lives. It's drilled into us from a young age. Like most things in life, there are pros and cons to everything. Comparing to others can take a sledgehammer to our self-esteem. When we see someone on a beach in Dubai, whilst you're stood on the train platform when it's pissing down with rain - it can make you feel like shit. The pressure to meet specific standards or compete with others can create a chronic state of tension, envy and even jealousy, impacting our mental and physical well-being. Real life is nuanced and imperfect; comparing yourself to idealised versions can result in disappointment and frustration. Continuous comparison can undermine your ability to find contentment in your own achievements and experiences. The pursuit of constantly "keeping up" with others may overshadow your genuine moments of joy. Trying to conform to others' lifestyles can result in abandoning your true self and adopting behaviours that are not aligned with your values.

But let's flip the coin. Comparing yourself to someone who has achieved what you aspire to can be a powerful motivator.

It can inspire you to set higher goals, work harder, and strive for personal excellence. Observing others who excel in a particular skill or field can provide valuable learning opportunities. Comparing your abilities to theirs can highlight areas for improvement and guide your efforts to enhance your skills by setting clear objectives and milestones for your own success. Comparing yourself to others can encourage our good old friend - self-reflection. Healthy competition can be a driving force for improvement. Seeking advice from individuals who have overcome obstacles can provide valuable insights and shortcuts to success.

We must be mindful of the negative impacts of constant comparison and strive to create a healthier relationship with ourselves. But it's equally important to approach comparison with a positive mindset and avoid destructive tendencies such as envy or constant self-criticism. The key is viewing comparisons as a tool for self-improvement and learning rather than as a means of validating self-worth. Balancing healthy comparison with self-compassion is crucial for maintaining a PMA, a positive mental attitude.

Avoiding constant comparison and adopting a more positive and inspirational approach to comparing yourself to others requires a combination of self-awareness, mindset shifts, and intentional practices. Goals, values and principles are the things that keep us grounded and make us self-aware. When you have a strong sense of your own path, you're less likely to be swayed by other peoples journeys that might be irrelevant. Recognising we're all on different paths is something we often forget. We're not all singing from the same hymn sheet, which makes life so exciting and vibrant. Look around you, whether you're reading this from a cafe, at home or on the bus. Everyone around you is on a different path. Everyone has different abilities and disabilities. Everyone has had various setbacks in life, and everyone's lives are on different speed settings. Treat yourself with the same compassion and understanding you would offer to a friend who's facing difficulties. Reflect on your own progress more than other people's, take note of the steps you've taken towards your goals and the obstacles you've overcome to motivate you to keep going. Another optimistic thing about comparison is that it can cultivate a habit of expressing gratitude. Regularly reflecting on the positive aspects of your life and accomplishments can shift your focus from what you lack to what you have, injecting your brain with positive vibes.

Someone once asked me: **Is life is a competition?** Thinking of the answer hurt my brain! What hurt even more is that I gave a politician's answer – the type of answer where you find yourself staring at the TV screen shouting, '**Just answer the fucking question'**!

The answer is yes and no. If you're continuously comparing yourself, looking at what car people have, how many bedrooms your friend's house has, that mate who's constantly dripping in designer clobber - then the answer is no. The answer is no because you're competing in a competition where the prize is someone else's life - a life where you probably only see the highlight reels. That's not competition; that's materialistic envy. But if you're always looking for ways to improve your life, making yourself feel good and doing things you love - then the answer is a big fat yes. Life is a competition, but you are the only competitor on the field. Of course, you can use comparison as a fuel for your tank - but make sure you're pumping the right fuel to avoid stalling, breakdowns, and wrong turns.

When someone says, "Get Over Yourself," they typically express the idea that the person should stop being so self-centred, self-absorbed, or self-important. It's an informal way of telling someone to stop being overly focused on their needs, opinions, or concerns and gain perspective or humility. This phrase is often used when someone is perceived as being excessively arrogant, egotistical, or overly concerned with their own interests to the detriment of others or the situation at hand. It's a suggestion to let go of excessive pride, self-importance, or a sense of entitlement and to adopt a more humble or considerate attitude.

Getting Over Yourself often requires a deliberate effort to control how much you compare yourself to others. Excessive comparison can hinder the journey towards self-discovery and authentic living, whether it leads to feelings of inadequacy or unwarranted supremacy. By actively moderating these comparisons, you preserve your self-worth and redirect your focus toward intrinsic motivations for personal growth. Getting Over Yourself involves breaking free from the cycle of seeking external validation and embracing a more authentic path. It's about setting and achieving goals that align with your values. As you navigate this process, you reduce unnecessary stress, build positive relationships based on collaboration rather than competition, and cultivate gratitude for the uniqueness of your own life. In essence, Getting Over Yourself entails controlling comparisons, transforming them from potential sources of detriment into tools for constructive self-reflection and individual development. It's a journey towards a healthier self-image, allowing you to embrace authenticity, purpose, and fulfilment on your own terms.

As we wrap up our exploration of comparison in this chapter, remember that the journey of self-discovery is uniquely yours, and comparisons should serve as guiding stars rather than stumbling blocks. The historical roots and scientific insights into social comparison provide a foundation for understanding this universal tendency. Acknowledging the pros and cons empowers us to navigate this terrain with wisdom.

In a world filled with influencers and societal benchmarks, let's pivot our focus to a healthier form of comparison. Seek inspiration from those who align with your mission and values, understanding that their success is not a benchmark but a testament to your journey's possibilities. Control the comparison by recognising that your path is distinct, and your progress is measured against your yesterday, not someone else's today.

As you close this chapter, carry with you the understanding that comparison can be a force for motivation and growth when directed inward. Like I said earlier, compare yourself to the person you were yesterday, not to others today. Let every comparison be a steppingstone in the direction of a more fulfilled and authentic version of yourself. Embrace the journey, celebrate your victories, and be inspired by the potential for positive change. As you look ahead, remember that the most significant competition is with the person you were, and the most inspiring influences are those that resonate with your authentic self. Your story is uniquely yours to craft, and the art of healthy comparison is a tool to shape a more purposeful tomorrow. Let's **KEEP IT REAL!**

Control The Comparison

FOOD FOR THOUGHT QUESTIONS ...

1) Reflect on when you felt genuine happiness or fulfilment without comparing yourself to others. What made that experience different?

2) How has comparing yourself to others influenced your self-esteem?

3) Reflect on instances when comparing yourself to others motivated positive change or growth. Conversely, when did it lead to negative outcomes?

CHAPTER 8
DON'T HATE, APPRECIATE

"APPRECIATION IS A THRIVING CURRENCY. THE MORE YOU SPEND IT, THE RICHER YOU BECOME"

There is one word that disrupts the harmony we seek: hate. Personally, I dislike many things. To name a few, I hate funerals, paying taxes, broccoli, and Instagram. This strong, four-letter word has wriggled its way into the fabric of our language, punctuating our sentences with intense heat that demands attention. But where did it come from, and why does it influence our modern discourse?

Let's do a 180 and trace the roots of "hate" back to Old English, where "hātian" meant to harbour intense or passionate dislike. Over time, this word has shape-shifted, morphing into a catch-all expression, flung casually at everything from inconveniences like Monday mornings to more significant issues. It's become a knee-jerk reaction to the challenges life often throws at us.

But what if we were to recalibrate our inner voice? What if we look at what we appreciate more often instead of falling back on the crutch of hate? Appreciation is not just a fluffy sentiment; it's a remedy for our souls. It's been scientifically proven that practising gratitude can improve our mental and physical health. Imagine starting your day not with a grumble about the weather (a favourite pastime of the British, I must say) but with a moment of appreciation for the world outside your window, whether it's the gentle rain tapping on the glass or the beaming sun making you sweat.

But, as mentioned previously, we humans are progress chasers. We often overlook the trivial things that give life its flavour — the first sip of a morning cuppa, the warmth of a shared joke, the reassuring touch of a loved one. These seemingly small moments are the building blocks of a fulfilling life, yet they can be drowned out in the racket of modern life. Appreciation is the art of tuning into these frequencies, recognising the beauty in the ordinary.

Recently, I was lucky enough to visit one of the most unique countries in the world - Cuba. History lesson alert - This nation has a rich and complex history. It was inhabited by indigenous people before the arrival of Christopher Columbus in 1492. Spanish colonisation followed, shaping Cuba's culture and society. In 1898, the Spanish-American War led to Cuba gaining independence from Spain, but it soon became a de facto U.S. protectorate. The mid-20th century saw political upheaval, with Fulgencio Batista coming to power. Fidel Castro and his revolutionaries overthrew Batista in 1959, establishing a socialist government. The Cold War tensions influenced Cuba's alignment with the Soviet Union, leading to the Cuban Missile Crisis in 1962. The U.S. imposed economic sanctions, also known as the embargo, exacerbating Cuba's financial challenges. After the collapse of the Soviet Union in 1991, Cuba faced a severe economic crisis, prompting limited market-oriented reforms in the 21st century.

Fast forwarding to now, the government has implemented

economic reforms to try and boost the economy, allowing minimal private enterprise whilst maintaining the illusion of a socialist political system. Tourism is the thing that puts money in the tills. Culture vultures head to the country to witness its fascinating history, classic cars, and stunning beaches. The death of Fidel Castro in 2016 marked a symbolic shift in leadership, with his brother Raúl Castro stepping down in 2018. Miguel Díaz-Canel assumed the presidency, representing a generational transition. Cuba's international relations have evolved. While maintaining strong ties with countries like Russia and China, there have been efforts to normalise relations with the United States. The country faces ongoing economic difficulties, intensified by the impact of the COVID-19 pandemic and the tightening of U.S. sanctions.

Whilst I admit my time there was to purely have fun and let my hair down, it healthily antagonised my thoughts. For most tourists, they see old American cars cruising through Havana, Cuban musicians tapping away on the bongos and people chomping away on cigars like there's no tomorrow. I thought this was the real Cuba - until I spoke to a few locals. My friend and I booked an experience called the Cuban trilogy - Coffee, Rum, and Cigars. We sat down with a local in a cafe, where he taught us how to properly smoke a cigar once we cleansed our palates with fresh coffee - washed down with a nice glass of neat Rum. We sat in the middle of the capital of Cuba, shooting the breeze with a gentleman who has lived through the Cuban revolution and beyond - and tapping into his thoughts was one of the most exciting things I've listened to in a while. It was when he said, 'I think most people want us to be colonised again,' that I chomped a little too much on my cigar and began coughing like a cat hacking up a hairball.

As I strolled through the vibrant streets of Havana, the spirit of appreciation enveloped me like a warm Caribbean breeze. The colourful exteriors, rhythmic music and warm smiles of the Cuban people painted a picture of resilience and unwavering positivity. Yet, beneath the surface, I discovered a profound lesson in appreciating life despite its challenges.

In Cuba, a country that has weathered economic storms and political uncertainties, food rationing is a stark reality. Every Cuban household is issued a Libreta de Abastecimiento, a ration book designed to ensure basic food staples for each family. While it guarantees a consistent supply of essential items, the quantities are often limited. Families must navigate their monthly allotments of rice, beans, sugar, and other necessities with ingenuity and resourcefulness. In Cuba, queues are not just a temporary inconvenience; they are a testament to the resilience of people accustomed to adapting. Access to money can be challenging, and Cubans line up at ATMs with a unique blend of patience and camaraderie.

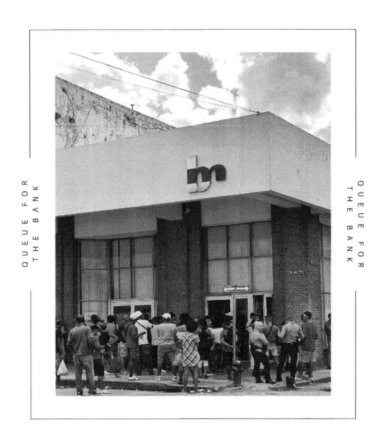

*Picture of people **queueing outside a bank** in central Havana,*
Cuba. A long wait to do something so simple.

While renowned for its emphasis on preventive care and medical diplomacy, the health system in Cuba faces limitations. Access to certain medicines and medical resources can be challenging due to economic constraints and international sanctions. Navigating economic opportunities in Cuba is a delicate dance. With a centralised economy, the avenues for opportunity and private enterprise are few and far between. The streets of Havana and other cities are decorated with vintage American cars, a picturesque reminder of a bygone era. While these classics evoke nostalgia and charm, they also massively contribute to air pollution. The sight of these enduring vehicles, held together with creativity and resourcefulness, pump out toxic fumes - meaning the air quality in populated cities like Havana is smoggy and thick.

As the wheels lifted off the tarmac at José Martí International Airport in Havana, I felt profound gratitude. The juxtaposition of the two worlds — the resilience of the Cuban people despite things like food shortages, and my own life with its relative abundance. It became a poignant reflection during the long journey back home.

In Cuba, access to certain medications can be a daily challenge. The lack of resources due to economic limitations and trade restrictions can make securing essential medicines complex. As I returned to a place where pharmacies are stocked with a vast array of medications, I found myself grateful for the seamless availability of essential drugs and treatments, often taken for granted in more economically prosperous nations.

Wandering the aisles of Cuban stores, I marvelled at the resourcefulness of the people making the most of limited options. Yet, the variety and abundance we enjoy in our supermarkets back home is a luxury that many Cubans can only dream of. The choices available to us, from fresh produce to gourmet delights, stand in stark contrast to the constrained selection faced by those in a country where rationing is a reality. Cuba's culinary scene is flavoured by simplicity, and the indulgence of a bar of chocolate can be a rare treat. As I sat on the plane, I unwrapped a piece of chocolate — a simple pleasure that spoke volumes. The realisation dawned that such small luxuries are commonplace in my daily life, a stark comparison to the scarcity experienced by many in Cuba.

With its vintage cars and charismatic charm, Havana also wears a shroud of exhaust fumes. The air, though vibrant with the city's energy, bears the pollution burden. As I touched down in a city with clearer skies, I inhaled deeply, appreciating the privilege of breathing air that, while not pristine, is far cleaner than Havana's hazy skies.

Navigating the bustling streets of Havana, I was amazed at the resourcefulness of Cubans using various modes of transport. However, the stark difference in accessibility hit me upon returning home. The convenience of an efficient public transportation system, with buses and trains crisscrossing the city, stood in contrast to the challenges faced by those reliant on more makeshift commuting methods.

As the aeroplane descended towards familiar territory, I couldn't help but reflect on the resilience and gratitude that define the Cuban spirit. Despite their challenges, the people of Cuba embrace life with a warmth and authenticity that leaves a lasting mark on those fortunate enough to witness it. And for me, returning home from this journey became more than a physical return; it became a profound reminder of the abundance that colours my daily life. This is a wake up call to savour the richness of what we have and, above all, to appreciate the simple joys that often escape us in the rat race of our fast-paced lives.

Beyond the idiosyncrasies of British weather and our stoic commitment to ignoring each other on the tube, there's much to be grateful for. According to the World Happiness Report, amongst the 195 countries that currently exist, the U.K. consistently ranks among the top 20 happiest countries globally. This leads me to ask why so many people see the glass half empty? Why is there so much negativity brewing in people? Have we lost our sense of gratefulness, or do we need to be more appreciative of what we have?

I'm not sitting here penning that life is a bed of roses. When you step back and look at life through a wide lens, there is much to be grateful about. In the U.K., we've been a democracy since 1832. Every five years, we head to the ballot box to decide whether to keep our current government or book the van removal company for Downing Street on behalf of the Prime Minister. We might not always like our government, and we have work to do to agree to disagree with each other healthily - but at least we have a chance to change it.

Just before the sun started to set on the 8th September 2022, news presenters graced our screens wearing black clothing as we were told the sad news that our Monarch for over 70 years had sadly died - turning Prince Charles into King Charles III. After the funeral of Queen Elizabeth, Prime Minister Liz Truss unveiled her mini-budget economic experiment, which led to her downfall and eventual resignation. Shortly after, Prime Minister Sunak strolled into number 10 to sail the ship. There is no denying that our economy took a hit, and people had a gloomy outlook on the events unfolding. But strangely - amongst all the change, panic, concern, and turmoil, it made me realise I'm grateful for our 'System'.

In the span of just 45 days, the United Kingdom experienced a whirlwind of significant events that underscored the resilience and stability of its political and institutional systems. Amidst the fast-paced changes, the British people witnessed a seamless transition of power and the continuity of governance, showcasing the strength of our democratic foundations.

Within this brief period, the U.K. saw not one but two

changes in its Prime Minister. Despite the political shifts, the transitions were executed with a remarkable degree of order and adherence to established protocols. The British parliamentary system demonstrated its capacity to accommodate leadership changes swiftly and efficiently, ensuring that the government continued to function without significant disruptions.

The passing of the Monarch marked a poignant moment for the nation. However, the grace and continuity of the British monarchy were evident in the seamless transition to the new King. The traditions and institutions surrounding the monarchy provided a stabilising force, offering a sense of continuity and historical resilience even in the face of change.

In recent years, we've seen such a diverse opinion pool on politicians and the royal family. With the monarchy, some see them as the bedrock of our country and the jewel in the British Crown. On the flip side, some will see them as dossers who live a luxury life off the British taxpayer's back. Notably, amidst these dynamic changes, the United Kingdom maintained a remarkable absence of civil unrest or coups. The adherence to the rule of law, respect for democratic principles, and the stability of institutions ensured that the nation weathered the storm without descending into chaos. The maturity of the political culture and the trust in established systems played a pivotal role in preventing any descent into turmoil. In essence, the events of these 45 days served as a testament to the robustness of the British system and institutions. The ability to navigate political changes, economic challenges, and royal transitions without succumbing to upheaval demonstrated the strength of the democratic fabric that binds the United Kingdom together. It made me proud to be British and grateful that we live in a country where gung-ho coups are not a reality.

We also have a national health service (NHS) that picks us up when we fall. Established in 1948, the NHS is a testament to the nation's commitment to providing universal healthcare for all. Conceived in the aftermath of World War II, the NHS was born out of a desire to create a system that would offer healthcare services free at the point of use, regardless of an individual's socioeconomic status. The creation of the NHS amalgamated various existing healthcare services into one comprehensive system, introducing the principle of free healthcare for every man, woman and child. The NHS was founded on the belief that good healthcare should be a right, not a privilege. During the 1950s, the NHS expanded its services by introducing vaccines and an increased focus on preventative care. The creation of new hospitals and advancements in medical technologies marked this era, contributing to improved healthcare outcomes for the population. In the 1970s, the NHS shifted its focus to community health services, emphasising care outside traditional hospital settings. This period saw the establishment of community health centres and a holistic approach to healthcare that extended beyond treating illnesses and instead started to promote overall health and well-being. The 1990s saw a renewed emphasis on modernisation and technology integration into healthcare delivery. The introduction of electronic patient records and advances in medical treatments reflected a commitment to keeping the NHS at the forefront of medical innovation. In the 21st century, the NHS faces new challenges, including an ageing population and increased demand for healthcare services. Despite these challenges, the NHS has continued to adapt and evolve. Investments in healthcare infrastructure, workforce training, and a commitment to patient-centred care have been pivotal in sustaining the NHS's mission.

I'm not writing this avoiding the challenges our health system in the U.K. faces. It needs to perform and transform in parallel. It requires good management, good people, better financial management, and training for the next generation of heroes. Without a doubt, there are problems that the people we elect need to fix. Prime Minister, if you're reading this, pull your bloody finger out, mate! But, despite the waiting lists, seeing staff overworked and underpaid, and A&E waiting times sometimes being longer than a flight to most European countries, there is much to be grateful for.

The NHS is a source of immense gratitude for us Brits. It provides healthcare services that are comprehensive, accessible, and free at the point of use. We're grateful for the NHS because it is a beacon of compassion and resilience. It has weathered challenges, adapted to changing circumstances, and is steadfastly committed to the nation's well-being. The NHS stands as a collective achievement, a symbol of unity and shared responsibility for the entire community's health.

In America, seen as the country that represents the free world, it's a very different story. The healthcare system in the United States is characterised by a combination of public and private providers. Unlike countries with universal healthcare, the U.S. does not have a single-payer system, and access to healthcare services often depends on insurance coverage or the ability to pay out of pocket. Many Americans receive healthcare coverage through employer-sponsored insurance, government programs like Medicaid and Medicare, or individual plans purchased on the private market. The Affordable Care Act (ACA) has expanded access to insurance for many, but a significant portion of the population remains uninsured. The cost of medical treatments and services can be substantial for those without insurance. The

U.S. has a fee-for-service model, meaning that providers charge fees for each service rendered. Without insurance, individuals are responsible for covering the entire cost of medical care.

- If you get breast cancer in the USA without insurance, it can cost you at **LEAST** $48,000

- Blood tests can cost anywhere between **$40** and **$3,000**

- An X-ray could cost you up to **$3,000**

- Insulin without insurance can cost anywhere between **$530 - $1,100**, and an asthma inhaler will cost at least **$60.** Bargain - **right?**

Around 92% of the population has some sort of insurance. But that means that 8% don't. If you take the population of the USA into account, that is around 26.5 million people who have no insurance. That is nearly the entire population of Australia. These people, who will most likely be at the low-income part of the scale, are hung out to dry - fending for themselves in their hour of need.

This is what makes me grateful. We all pay our taxes that fund the NHS, so it's not entirely free, but it's there to catch us when we fall. Our NHS is an institution that reflects the core values of the United Kingdom, reminding us that in times of illness and adversity, we are not alone and we have a healthcare system built on the principle that health is a fundamental right for all.

Then there are our supermarkets, pharmacies, and corner shops. In my 30 years of existence, the only time I have seen shelves empty is when the toilet roll brigade raided the supermarkets at the start of the COVID-19 pandemic. We have an array of choices when it comes to food. We have food of different qualities, quantities, and costs. It makes me grateful for the factory workers, the butchers, the bakers, the shelf stackers and the lorry drivers who land the food on our plates. Paracetamol, ibuprofen, and other essential medical supplies are not in short supply. We have access to supplies that can keep headaches at bay, stamp out the pain, and keep the coughs on the down low. It seems trivial, but these are things that we should be grateful for - because it's something we often take for granted. I don't want to lecture us on absolutely everything we should be grateful for – I'm confident that we're all thankful for different things in life. But I want us to munch away on some food for thought and consider the things we're grateful for in life.

I'm thankful for Sun cream because I'm pasty and turn medium rare when it's over 25 degrees. I'm grateful for ATMs and contactless payments as it makes it easy for me to buy things. I appreciate books because they help me zone out and learn new things. I'm grateful for British humour - unmatched compared to anywhere else on Earth.

Should we be walking around daily thinking about what we are thankful for? The textbook answer is yes, of course we should! But we all know that life sometimes gets in the way of things. As mentioned previously in this book, self-reflection is essential. Reflecting on what you're grateful for is one of the critical ingredients for a big fat slice of 'Get Over Yourself ' pie.

Practising gratitude draws in numerous benefits for mental and emotional well-being. It has been correlated with reduced symptoms of depression and anxiety, heightened positive emotions and increased life satisfaction - even though that is pretty hard to measure. Gratitude is a stress buffer, enhancing resilience and coping mechanisms during challenging times. Additional advantages include strengthening relationships, being more empathetic, and contributing to better sleep quality - and who doesn't love better quality sleep?

Physically, gratitude is associated with lower blood pressure, improved immune function, and overall health. By focusing on the positives, individuals often experience heightened self-esteem and an increased desire to give back to others. The cognitive benefits include improved focus, productivity, and a positive impact on decision-making. Ultimately, cultivating gratitude contributes to long-term happiness and a more fulfilling life - and it could be as easy as thinking about something you're grateful for before you turn off the light at night.

A lot of dislike and hate is stitched into the fabric of our modern lives. But alongside that, a simple yet powerful thread weaves through that very same fabric — the thread of gratitude. It gently reminds us not to harbour resentment but to appreciate what we have. As we navigate the complexities of our daily lives, it's easy to be pulled into the undertow of discontent, comparing ourselves to others or fixating on what's lacking. However, within the quiet act of acknowledging the positives lies the transformative force of gratitude. Gratitude isn't a call to settle or an invitation to become complacent. It's about opening our eyes to the richness of our present reality and finding beauty in the everyday. This mindset becomes a guiding light, steering us from resentment and self-pity toward a place of contentment. But let's not mistake gratitude for a force that stifles our ambitions. It's a harmonious companion to our dreams, reminding us that it's okay to desire more and strive for a better future. The key is moderation — reaching for the stars while staying grounded.

My friends, let's step down from the pedestals we sometimes perch upon — pedestals built from resentment and entitlement. Let's feel the solid ground beneath our feet, not as a limitation but as a foundation to make our dreams. The path to a fulfilled existence lies in this balanced reality, where we embrace lofty aspirations and the simple joys of today. It's a journey that requires introspection, a pause in the relentless pursuit of more, and a mindful recognition of the beauty in ordinary moments.

Let's redefine our narrative in a world often fixated on what's lacking. Let's choose to appreciate the present, finding joy in the most minor details. In this appreciation, we unlock the true essence of a fulfilling and simplistic life - a life where we truly Get Over Ourselves.

Don't Hate, Appreciate

FOOD FOR THOUGHT QUESTIONS ...

1) Consider your relationships, work, and personal experiences. What are you grateful for right now?

2) When was the last time you expressed appreciation to someone in your life? What was their reaction?

3) How can you make a conscious effort to express gratitude more regularly?

CHAPTER 9

BE KIND

"KINDNESS IS A GIFT THAT EVERYONE CAN AFFORD TO GIVE"

The history of kindness is a tale as old as humanity itself. While pinpointing the first act of kindness in the chronicles of time is pretty much impossible, i can imagine early humans extending a helping hand or sharing resources as a form of communal survival.

In ancient cultures, kindness often found expression in religious or philosophical teachings. As societies evolved, so did the manifestations of kindness. The Middle Ages saw the rise of chivalry, where knights adhered to a code of conduct that included acts of kindness and protection, especially towards the weak and vulnerable. During the Renaissance, the concept of civility emerged, highlighting the importance of gracious behaviour and consideration for others in social interactions.

In the 19th and 20th centuries, movements for social justice often drew strength from the principles of kindness and empathy. Inspired by figures like Florence Nightingale and Mahatma Gandhi, humanitarian efforts highlighted compassion's transformative power in addressing societal challenges.

In the post-World War II period, we witnessed a surge in global initiatives aimed at increasing kindness and cooperation, with the establishment of organisations like the United Nations dedicated to promoting peace and understanding among nations. The rebuilding of Britain was marked by a collective spirit of kindness and shared purpose. While it would be simplistic to attribute the recovery solely to kindness, elements of compassion, empathy, and community played integral roles. The Labour government, elected in 1945, implemented social reforms that established the foundation for the modern welfare state, complimented by the creation of the National Health Service in 1948. Communities, forged through the shared experience of war, demonstrated solidarity in rebuilding efforts, with acts of kindness and mutual support. International aid, such as the Marshall Plan, exemplified global cooperation in reconstruction. Moreover, investments in education and innovation reflected a compassionate commitment to equipping the population with the skills needed for recovery.

In the contemporary landscape, the essence of kindness has evolved to encompass not only individual deeds but also sweeping changes in systems and society. The digital age presents a stage where kindness faces both daunting challenges and promising opportunities. Online movements and social media campaigns passionately rally for positive change and collective support. Yet, amidst the virtual realms, lurking trolls emerge as keyboard warriors, unleashing waves of negativity that threaten the very fabric of goodwill.

Kindness is a rich virtue that encompasses a variety of positive qualities and behaviours. At its core, kind individuals deeply understand and share feelings with others, showing empathy. They go beyond awareness, actively desiring to ease the suffering of those around them, displaying genuine compassion. Generosity is another key aspect, as they willingly give and help without expecting anything in return. Patience and under-standing define their interactions, especially in tough situations, where they provide others the needed time and space to express themselves or overcome challenges.

Respecting others is fundamental to kindness, involving treating everyone with courtesy, consideration and recognising the dignity and autonomy of each person. Kind individuals ra-diate positivity, focusing on uplifting aspects of situations and openly expressing gratitude for others' efforts. Acts of helpful-ness, an open-minded and accepting attitude, humility, and for-giveness are also linked to kindness. They offer encouragement and support, inspiring others to achieve their goals and engage in selfless acts for the well-being of others.

Guided by integrity and consistent values, kind individuals engage in active listening, validating the feelings and experienc-es of those around them. By cultivating these traits, individuals contribute to a kind and compassionate approach to interperson-al relationships and the broader community, giving a positive and supportive environment for everyone involved. It reflects our natural understanding that, regardless of the passage of time, kindness remains a timeless and universal virtue, bringing us together in our shared human journey.

Do you ever remember where you were when certain people passed away? These are called 'Flashbulb' moments. I always remember where I was and what I was doing when Michael Jackson, Amy Winehouse and Whitney Houston died. A flash-bulb moment is a highly detailed and vivid memory associat-ed with a significant event. These memories are often linked to events that hold emotional and cultural importance. People tend to remember specific details, such as their location and activities during the event, as if a mental "flashbulb" captured the moment.

In Christmas 2019, because of our mutual interest in politics, I treated my Nan to a Christmas gift – tickets to the play 'The Last Temptation of Boris Johnson.' We went to the show on the 15th February 2020. As the interval unfolded and the sweet melody of the ice cream sellers filled the theatre, I glanced at my phone to find a news notification delivering the sad news of Caroline Flack's passing. Caroline, the presenter of one of my favourite shows, had left us. Checking my phone after the show, it revealed the heart-breaking truth: Caroline Flack had taken her own life.

Caroline Flack, the vibrant presenter of Love Island, faced tumultuous times in the months leading to her tragic passing. She was entangled in a complex situation involving an ongoing police investigation related to an incident with her boyfriend. This legal scrutiny had consequences beyond the personal sphere, and she was replaced as the host of Love Island.

Amidst the public spotlight and her challenges, Caroline posted a poignant message on her Instagram: "In a world where you can be anything, be kind." Little did anyone know that these words would echo profoundly in the aftermath of her passing.

The phrase "Be Kind" soon transcended a mere caption on social media. It became a rallying cry, a reminder that behind every public persona is a person grappling with their own struggles. In a world increasingly dominated by digital interactions, this simple yet profound mantra urged people to reconsider the impact of their words, both online and offline.

Caroline Flack's tragic end ignited a collective reflection on the harshness of public scrutiny, the consequences of judgment, and the toll that unrelenting media attention can take on an individual's mental health. The phrase "Be Kind" transformed into a powerful legacy, encouraging compassion and empathy as antidotes to the often unforgiving nature of the world.

In the wake of her passing, conversations about mental health, the importance of supportive communities, and the need for kindness gained renewed prominence. Caroline Flack's legacy is a poignant reminder that everyone is fighting their battles behind the glamour of fame or veneer of success. The call to "Be Kind" resonates as a beacon, urging us to approach one another with compassion, understanding, and a recognition of our shared humanity. As we navigate complex challenges and profound societal shifts, we need more kindness now than ever before.

In an interconnected world where information spreads rapidly, individual actions reverberate globally. Acts of kindness can bridge divides, spread empathy, and build stronger communities. As we face unprecedented challenges, from public health crises to environmental concerns, the need for collective goodwill becomes paramount.

The concept that kindness comes in different sizes emphasises that it could be everyday gestures to grand, impactful deeds. Both types of kindness contribute to positive experiences and make a difference in people's lives. It does not always have to be big gestures like donating to charity, volunteering your time or taking your damsel in distress friend for a coffee. A simple smile can brighten someone's day and create a positive ripple effect. It's a small gesture, but it has the power to uplift spirits and promote a sense of connection. Offering a genuine compliment to a colleague about their work or attitude is a small act of kindness that can boost morale and create a more positive and supportive work environment. Even holding the door open for someone behind you is a common and small act of courtesy. It may seem trivial, but it reflects thoughtfulness and consideration for others.

The beauty of the concept lies in its diversity —it acknowledges that not all acts of kindness need to be grand or elaborate to be meaningful. Small acts woven into the fabric of daily life can accumulate and spread good vibes. At the same time, more significant acts have the potential to bring about transformative change and address systemic issues. Recognising and appreciating the spectrum of kindness encourages people to embrace opportunities to make a positive impact, regardless of the scale of the gesture.

Kindness is a remedy for the isolation that modern life can breed. In an era dominated by digital interactions, where screens often mediate our connections, simple acts of kindness bring a genuine human touch. Whether it's a supportive message, a helping hand, or a smile, these gestures counteract the potential alienation inherent in our increasingly virtual existence.

Moreover, kindness is a powerful antidote to the negativity that can fuel public discourse. It challenges the culture of divisiveness and encourages dialogue. In a time when opinions can be polarised, understanding and kindness pave the way for constructive conversations and collaborative problem-solving.

In essence, kindness is not just a nicety; it's a fundamental force that can shape the trajectory of our shared future. It brings light to the darkest corners of our world, offering hope and resilience. Now, as we confront unprecedented global challenges, the importance of kindness transcends sentimentality; it becomes a practical and indispensable tool for building a more compassionate, understanding, and interconnected world. When you extend kindness, it often instils a sense of fulfilment and joy within yourself. Making someone else's day brighter, even in a small way, can bring a deep sense of satisfaction.

In the early days of my working life, I started as an IT Apprentice for a utility company. During that time, my manager,

Kathy, shared something with me that has stayed in my mind ever since. She had recently lost her father, and she passed on a quote that he always used to tell her: "People will always forget what you said and what you did, but they will never forget how you made them feel." To me, this perfectly captures the enduring impact of kindness. Words may fade, and actions may blur over time, but the emotions you stir in others last forever. Acts of kindness leave a lasting imprint on people.

Moreover, kindness has tangible benefits for mental and emotional well-being. Scientific studies show that engaging in acts of kindness triggers the release of feel-good hormones, such as oxytocin. This enhances your mood and contributes to stress reduction and an overall sense of happiness.

Kindness contributes to creating supportive and compassionate communities in a broader societal context. It strengthens social bonds and builds a foundation of trust. As individuals experience kindness, they are more likely to pay it forward, creating a cycle of positivity that can permeate entire communities.

The term "Pay It Forward" gained popularity through the 2000 film called Pay It Forward, directed by Mimi Leder and based on the novel by Catherine Ryan Hyde. In the movie, a young lad starts a movement of doing good deeds for others without expecting anything in return, with the hope that the recipients will then do the same for someone else.

The Pay It Forward movement has inspired various real-life initiatives and experiments where people are encouraged to perform acts of kindness for strangers, friends, or family members. These acts can range from simple gestures like paying for someone's coffee or meal to more significant actions like helping someone in need or volunteering time for a charitable cause.

On the night of May 22, 2017, the Manchester Arena, usually a place of joy and music, witnessed a devastating turn of events. An Ariana Grande concert, filled with fans, families, and music enthusiasts, became the target of a terrorist attack. A suicide bomber detonated an explosive device, taking the lives of 22 innocent people and leaving scores more with physical injuries and emotional scars that will last a lifetime.

In the wake of this tragic incident, a powerful counter-narrative emerged amongst the chaos and anguish—one driven by kindness and resilience. As the echoes of the explosion still reverberated, acts of compassion became the guiding light in the darkness.

One remarkable display of kindness unfolded through the city's taxi drivers. Instead of fleeing the scene, they lined the streets, offering free rides to those affected by the attack. In their simple yet profound gesture, these drivers became the unsung heroes of the night, providing not just transportation but a sense of security and solidarity for those affected.

Emergency services were stretched to their limits, and in the face of this crisis, ordinary citizens opened their doors to strangers. Homes became sanctuaries, places where people found refuge and solace amongst all the panic and uncertainty. The kindness of those individuals transformed the city into a community bound together by shared pain and mutual support.

The hospitals, inundated with the injured, became hubs of compassion. Medical professionals worked tirelessly, not just to treat physical wounds but to offer emotional support to those grappling with the trauma. The acts of kindness in the hospital corridors, from healthcare professionals and volunteers alike, demonstrated that even in the darkest times, the human spirit could shine brightly.

The resilience of the people of Manchester, coupled with

these acts of kindness, showcased an unwavering commitment to unity and compassion. The city refused to be defined solely by the tragedy; instead, it rallied around the principles of solidarity and love. The northern grit and determination of the Mancunians came out in full force.

This tragic night, marred by senseless violence, became a testament to the enduring power of kindness. It illustrated that even in the face of unimaginable horror, humanity could rise above hatred and division. The collective response demonstrated that kindness can prevail and become the force that makes the world go round. In the aftermath of tragedy, these acts of compassion stand as beacons of hope, guiding communities toward healing and rebuilding.

Kindness serves as a valuable currency in the complex economy of human interactions. Like money, kindness facilitates positive exchanges which creates trust and goodwill between different people. Acts of kindness act as investments, yielding returns that benefit both the giver and the recipient. This universal currency transcends cultural and societal boundaries, fostering connections and understanding. The idea of kindness as currency aligns seamlessly with the philosophy of karma, where kind acts contribute to a positive karmic cycle in accordance with the law of reciprocity. Engaging in acts of kindness accumulates positive karma, fostering qualities like empathy and compassion and contributing to personal growth. The ripple effect of kindness extends beyond immediate transactions, influencing the interconnected web of human experiences. Unlike material currencies, kindness holds a unique place as a currency of the heart, measured in the intangible warmth, connection, and joy it brings us.

While the magic of kindness radiates positive energy, a

few mischievous elements might sneak into the mix. Excessive goodwill attracts the beings of exploitation, as some individuals might take advantage of peoples generosity. Striking a balance in acts of kindness, however, can be like walking on a tightrope; the constant juggling may result in a circus of burnout and neglect of our own desires. Watch out for these mischievous elements, as they play tricks with boundaries, adding an element of mystery like a disappearing act.

Sometimes, digging deep and being the bigger person is difficult. It requires you to be the better person, despite you wanting to throttle the person who's being a twat to you. But, sometimes, your secret weapon is kindness. "Kill them with kindness" is an expression advocating the response to negativity, criticism, or hostility with kindness and positivity rather than with a similarly negative attitude. The essence lies in disarming or winning over adversaries, critics, or challenging individuals through an unexpected, gentle, or considerate response. Proponents of this approach believe that choosing kindness can defuse tension, promote understanding, and alter the dynamics of an interaction.

The effectiveness of "kill them with kindness" can be attributed to several factors:

- Responding with kindness catches the other party off guard, making it more challenging for them to maintain a hostile stance.

- Kindness can shift the overall tone of a conversation or relationship, creating a more positive and constructive atmosphere.

- By responding with kindness, individuals set an example of the behaviour they would like to see in return, potentially influencing the other party to reconsider their approach. This approach also helps break the cycle of escalation that often accompanies responding to aggression with more of the same.

- Choosing kindness can be a form of self-preservation, as responding in a hostile manner can contribute to stress and emotional distress.

However, it's crucial to recognise that "killing someone with kindness" is not a universal solution and may not be appropriate in all situations. In some instances, assertiveness, setting boundaries, or addressing issues firmly is more effective. Additionally, the concept does not imply naivety or passive acceptance of mistreatment; instead, it suggests responding to negativity to promote a positive and constructive outcome. You're circulating that kindness currency and getting more bang for your buck!

Kindness emerges as a transformative force to help individuals break free from self-centred perspectives and truly "Get Over Themselves." By actively engaging in acts of kindness, people can shift their focus away from personal concerns and immerse themselves in the well-being and experiences of others. This intentional shift cultivates empathy, fostering a profound connection to the larger human experience. Kindness, in its essence, encourages individuals to rise above self-centred thoughts, promoting a sense of community and shared humanity.

Recall a moment when someone's kindness lit up your day like a burst of sunshine breaking through the clouds. It could have been a genuine smile from a stranger, a friend lending a listening ear, or a small yet significant gesture that spoke volumes. These bursts of kindness are like tiny fireworks of warmth and possess the power to transform not just a moment but an entire day, week, or even a lifetime.

Now, consider a time when you may have strayed from kindness, when the demands of life or the hustle and bustle clouded your ability to be gentle with others. It's a common occurrence, and rather than dwelling on self-judgment, let's use these moments as steppingstones to growth.

Kindness, in all its manifestations, is the heartbeat of a thriving, interconnected world. It transcends borders, cultures, and generations, serving as the universal language that resonates in the symphony of shared humanity. As we navigate our way through life, let's be mindful of the steps we take, the ripples we create, and the energy we contribute to the world.

Let's not just discuss kindness but embody it in every interaction, both in the digital landscapes of social media and the tangible canvas of our daily lives. Let's become architects of joy, painters of compassion, and conductors of harmony. For in being kind, we illuminate our own path and cast a warm glow that lights the way for others.

FOOD FOR THOUGHT QUESTIONS ...

1) Can you recall a personal experience where someone's kindness made a significant difference in your day or life? What happened?

2) Reflect on a time when you witnessed or experienced unkindness. How did it make you feel, and what could have been done differently?

3) In what ways can small acts of kindness create a ripple effect in a society?

CHAPTER 10
DON'T DROP YOU MORAL COMPASS

"WITHOUT A MORAL COMPASS, THE HUMAN MIND WILL JUSTIFY ANYTHING"

In our complicated lives, where the lines between right and wrong sometimes blur and opinions drown out the whispers of conscience, we occasionally find ourselves navigating challenging terrain. Morals, values, and principles act as our compass, pointing us towards the true north star of our authentic selves. At the start of this book, I spoke about society sometimes being like a compass gone haywire in an era of unparalleled comforts and opportunities. This chapter is a reminder, a call to arms, to cherish and safeguard our moral compasses — those silent guides that shape our actions and define our character.

Morals, principles, and values are interrelated concepts that shape an individual's ethical framework. Morals are deeply personal, representing an individual's internal compass of right and wrong, often influenced by upbringing, culture, and unique experiences. Principles, on the other hand, are foundational truths or guidelines derived from ethical or philosophical sources, providing a broader framework for decision-making. Values encompass a range of beliefs and standards that individuals find important, influencing their attitudes and choices. In this analogy, if morals are the essential pocket watch one always carries, values and principles can be likened to the intricate hands on the clock. Values and principles underpin and guide morals, providing a structured foundation for the individual's ethical perspective and influencing the decisions and actions derived from their moral compass. Together, these elements form a comprehensive system that navigates the complex landscape of human behaviour and ethical reasoning.

To understand the significance of our moral compass, we must first unravel the history of human morality. From ancient philosophies to religious beliefs, our understanding of right and wrong has evolved across cultures. Public executions in the UK, once deemed a legitimate form of justice, now stand as a stark reminder of the evolution of our moral consciousness. In past eras, a public execution was a communal event believed to serve justice and deter crime. Today, most people recoil at the very idea, recognising the brutality and inhumanity of such acts. What can we learn from the moral beacons of history? How have these guiding lights influenced societies and individuals?

Consider the transformation in societal attitudes towards same-sex relationships. In the not-so-distant past, being gay was considered immoral, a view still held by many cultures around the world. Individuals who dared to love against conventional norms faced persecution and discrimination and often lived in fear. Fast forward to the present, and many societies now celebrate love in all its forms, recognising the right of individuals to express their affections freely.

Similarly, the issue of gender equality highlights a shift in our moral landscape. Throughout history, women were denied fundamental rights and opportunities and relegated to subordinate roles. Today, women are smashing their way through the glass ceilings - taking on some of the most critical roles in society.

There has been a notable shift in values in recent years, particularly among younger generations. There is an increased emphasis on prioritising life experiences over traditional markers of success, focusing on travel, personal growth, and meaningful connections. Technology and social media have shaped global perspectives, promoted connectivity, and raised awareness of societal issues. Environmental consciousness, diversity, inclusion, and a commitment to work-life balance are vital themes shaping contemporary values.

Religion has historically served as a powerful moral compass for individuals worldwide. Major world religions provide followers with a structured ethical framework through sacred texts, commandments, and moral teachings. These teachings often include narratives stories that convey moral lessons, helping individuals understand the good, the bad and the ugly. This helps people understand the consequences of their actions. Religious communities offer a shared space where individuals uphold moral values through rituals, gatherings, and ceremonies - stimulating moral unity. Additionally, religion guides ethical decision-making, providing believers with principles to navigate complex moral dilemmas. The belief in accountability to a higher power acts as a deterrent against immoral behaviour, reinforcing adherence to ethical standards. Religion also provides a sense of purpose and meaning, encouraging moral development and personal growth through rituals and spiritual practices. While the impact of religion on an individual's moral compass varies, it remains a significant influence on peoples perspective and behaviours.

Rosa Parks, often called the "Mother of the Civil Rights Movement," played a massive role in challenging racial segregation in the United States. Her act of civil disobedience in De-

cember 1955 became a catalyst for the Montgomery Bus Boycott and marked a significant turning point in the fight against
racial injustice.

On that fateful day in December, Rosa Parks, a 42-year-old
African American seamstress, boarded a Montgomery city bus
in Alabama after a long day at work. According to the segregation laws of the time, the bus had designated sections for white
and black passengers, with the front reserved for white passengers and the back for black passengers. When the white section
of the bus filled up, the bus driver demanded that Parks and three
other African American passengers give up their seats to white
passengers. Unlike the prevailing practice where African Americans were expected to comply with such demands, Rosa Parks
refused to give up her seat. Her refusal was not impulsive; it was
a deliberate and principled act of civil disobedience. Parks was
well aware of the systemic racism and segregation in her community, and she had been a member of the NAACP (National
Association for the Advancement of Coloured People) for years.

Parks' decision was a result of her strong moral convictions
and her commitment to challenging the unjust racial segregation
laws. Her act was not only a personal stand but a strategic move
to contribute to the larger struggle of Black people in America.
Parks later said, "People always say that I didn't give up my seat
because I was tired, but that isn't true. I was not tired physically,
or no more tired than I usually was at the end of a working day.
I was not old, although some people have an image of me as
being old then. I was 42. No, the only tired I was was tired of
giving in."

The arrest of Rosa Parks led to a citywide boycott of Montgomery buses organised by local civil rights leaders, including
a young minister named Martin Luther King Jr. The boycott,

known as the Montgomery Bus Boycott, lasted for 381 days and was a significant turning point in the civil rights movement. The Supreme Court eventually ruled that segregation on public buses was unconstitutional, officially ending the Montgomery Bus Boycott.

Rosa Parks' courageous act and the subsequent boycott demonstrated the power of nonviolent resistance and civil disobedience in the face of racial injustice. Her moral stand resonated nationally and internationally, bringing attention to the struggles of black people and inspiring a generation of civil rights activists. Rosa Parks' actions, driven by her unwavering moral compass, helped kickstart a societal shift in attitudes toward race and contributed to the broader movement for civil rights in the United States and across the world.

The thing is, our world is continuously changing. In the last 50 years, we've seen massive changes. 50 years ago, personal computers were in their infancy, and the internet was yet to be developed. Now, the world is digitally connected, with smartphones, high-speed internet, social media, and advanced computing technologies. Diseases like smallpox were still common, but fast forwards 50 years, there have been considerable advancements in vaccines, organ transplants, gene therapy, and other medicines. Concerns about the environment were emerging, but widespread awareness and global initiatives were limited - compared to now, where it's on the desk of every person in power. These changes indicate that our moral compass needs to be adaptable. If everyone had the same moral compass, underpinned by the same values and principles forever - we'd be stuck in the dark ages. So, whilst having a moral compass is incredibly powerful to help us navigate the choppy seas of life, we must listen, be willing to reassess and be open to change. If Rosa Parks didn't stick to her guns - the societal change could have taken much longer than it did.

Even though I've named this chapter Don't Drop Your Moral Compass, many people - don't even have one to drop, or it's in a drawer collecting dust somewhere. I'm not speaking about a physical compass here; I'm talking about understanding who we are and our principles and values. In job interviews, one question that's always asked is, 'So, tell me about yourself'. It's the question that usually throws people off. More often than not, it's responded to with something like, 'I'm Gary, I'm a Project Manager and I like hiking, golfing and watching the footie down the pub with my mates.' I'm not saying that's a wrong answer, but it only tells a small part of the story. Who is the real Gary? You don't want to go into a 'This is your life' moment with the person interviewing you, but a big chunk of people don't even touch on their values and principles - because they don't know what they are. Do you know yours?

Understanding our values and principles is crucial for navigating life with purpose and authenticity. These core beliefs serve as a guiding compass, helping us make decisions aligned with our deeply held convictions. By grasping our values, we can set priorities, allocate resources, and build a fulfilling and meaningful life. Living and breathing our values reduces internal conflict and stress whilst implementing a sense of authenticity and inner peace. Also, shared values form the basis of strong personal and professional relationships, allowing us to connect with like-minded people. In the workplace, understanding our values guides our career choices and behaviour, contributing to professional success and satisfaction. Principles derived from these values provide a flexible framework for ethical decision-making, allowing for adaptability and growth over time.

In times of crisis, knowing our values offers stability and resilience. Ultimately, this self-awareness contributes to our well-being and inspires a sense of responsibility to contribute to society, creating positive vibes all around.

So, how on earth do we even start to understand our principles and values? Well, let's bring back our trusty friend - self-reflection. Taking the time to self-reflect is like taking a closer look at yourself. We spend so much time zooming in on pictures of ourselves and self-critiquing our looks - so why don't we do this with our cognitive thinking? Self-reflection is thinking about how you feel, what you've been through, and how you act. When you reflect, you try to understand why and how you do certain things that affect you and others. It's like asking yourself questions to determine what's important to you and how to improve on the person you were yesterday. It helps you learn more about who you are and why you do the things you do.

Do we pay enough attention to how we react to things? Our feelings can provide clues about what matters to us deeply. Ask yourself why you feel a certain way in specific circumstances. When and what makes you smile, laugh, angry and emotional? Why does it make you feel like that?

Role models serve as examples or sources of inspiration for our values and principles. They embody qualities, values, and behaviours admired and worth reliving. Role models can be found in daily life - family, friends, teachers, celebrities, or community leaders. They are crucial in shaping our aspirations, beliefs, and behaviours. Self-reflection is mainly about you but also about what influences you and how other people make you feel.

Life can be viewed as one big negotiation where we continuously engage in decision-making, compromise, and adaptation. Setting and pursuing goals, whether in education, career, or personal development, involves negotiation with ourselves and others. Relationships, both personal and professional, require decent communication and compromise. Career development includes negotiations on salary, contracts, and collaborations. Decision-making is a constant negotiation between priorities and values, and adaptation to change involves negotiation with evolving circumstances. Imagine you've taken the time to reflect on your values and principles, considering what truly matters to you. By doing this, you've identified what is most and least important in your life. These insights are valuable because they guide us in negotiating our boundaries—helping us determine what we're willing to accept, what we can tolerate, and what we prefer to avoid altogether.

But as well as negotiating choice, there is also the topic of how we deal with moral dilemmas. A moral dilemma is when we face a difficult choice between two or more options, and each option involves conflicting moral principles or values. In other words, no matter what decision is made, it seems to involve a violation of a moral principle, and there is no silver bullet when it comes to providing an answer. For example, a moral dilemma might involve someone choosing between telling the truth and potentially hurting someone or lying to protect someone's feelings. The dilemma arises from the conflicting values of honesty and compassion, making it difficult to determine the most morally justifiable course of action.

Moral dilemmas often create a sense of ethical conflict and may require individuals to weigh up the consequences of their actions and consider the ethical implications. They are challenging because they involve competing values, and making a decision may require individuals to prioritise one principle over another. These situations are complex and can make us feel like shit! When we find ourselves in a tricky situation where it's hard to decide what's right, it's hard to think about how to deal with the situation. Understanding the facts can consider how different choices lead to different outcomes. Think about what's important to you in this situation - this is where it's convenient to know what your values and principles are.

Regularly reassessing our values and principles is a key ingredient for growth and adapting to the ever-changing dynamics of society. As individuals evolve through experiences, reassessment ensures that our values align with our current beliefs and aspirations. Considering societal changes, reassessing values helps individuals adapt to cultural shifts and external influences. Ultimately, this ongoing process contributes to a more intentional, fulfilling, and authentic life - something that we're all here for.

Before going any further, I'm going to fess up. We're all guilty of dropping our moral compass at some point. I would personally say my values are empathy, calmness, awareness, and respect. Underpinned by the principles of active listening, adaptability, and balance.

Here's a little tale from my part-time job at a coffee shop during the festive season in my late teens. Mariah Carey's christmas tunes were humming in the background, and the Christmas lights turned our coffee machine into a makeshift disco ball. I was in the zone, whipping up what I considered the world's best cappuccinos, lattes, and hot chocolates. Meanwhile, my colleague Monika was handling orders at the till.

Picture this: A short, red-faced guy sporting a flat cap walks in, ready for his caffeine fix. I'm doing the coffee hustle, Monika's taking orders, and everything's buzzing. Monika was from

Poland - her English was not perfect, but she had a heart of gold and a temper of steel. We were dealing with hundreds of orders every hour, so it was only a matter of time before we got an order wrong.

I served the short red-faced bloke his coffee and said Enjoy! However, either Monika had forgotten to tell me, or I didn't hear - but he wanted his coffee with skimmed milk. It wasn't a biggy, a simple mistake but could easily be rectified.

However, you'd think Monika had committed mass murder because the customer exploded into fit of rage. I thought my ears needed cleaning out - because I heard him say 'Fucking foreigners, can't get anything right!'. I should have refunded him his money and politely asked him to leave - remaining calm and resolute.

This is where it all goes out the window. Instead of playing it cool, I make a questionable choice. I tell him to take a seat and promise to bring his drink over. In the process of remaking his coffee, I sniffed my nose and spat in his drink. Merry Christmas, idiot! I must admit, this was not my finest hour, but how dare he say that! With hindsight, I should of dealt with it in a better way and not stooped to a pathetic new low.

Cut to today, and you're probably thinking, "Really, Jack?" Yeah, spitting in someone's coffee is not my proudest move. While I can't say I feel particularly sorry for that guy, I do regret my less-than-impressive reaction. In a way, I'm glad it happened as it now constantly reminds me to be calm and be the bigger person. I regret it, but it's a lesson learned: Keep that moral compass close and avoid coffee shop drama at all costs.

I've recently sat down and thought about what the world could be like in the next 50 years. When I look back at history, the world looked and felt extremely different. So, in the latter half of this century, when I'm probably drinking out of a straw or dead and buried - the world will most likely be beyond recognition compared to what we know today.

Reflecting on historical movements such as the Montgomery bus boycott, the Suffragettes movement, and the Apartheid Resistance, I appreciate the people who followed their moral compass. They managed to bring about significant change. However, when I observe some present-day movements like Extinction Rebellion disrupting traffic and people advocating for pronoun usage, I can't help but feel that the world is becoming increasingly unorthodox. I'm not alone; many share the belief that the world is going mad. But an intriguing consideration keeps popping into my head: What if this unconventional path is the future? What if these movements are right, bringing about a dawn of a new era, and I find myself resistant to change?

Debates in modern society are too heated and argumentative - people get triggered too quickly, leaving their sense of calm at the door when they walk into a room. Of course, if someone gets up in your grill demanding you drive an electric car, or eat mungbean salads for breakfast, lunch and dinner whilst referring to themselves as they/them - it would be hard not to shout FUCK OFF at the top of your voice. Remaining calm is essential to navigating your moral compass because it allows for thoughtful and rational decision-making in the face of challenging situations.

Everyone in this world is different, but we should encourage ourselves to be differently united and reduce the temperature of these debates to allow healthy discussion. An old saying is you learn something new every day - which is probably right. Education on both sides of any debate is crucial, but it requires us to listen just as much as it requires us to speak. If we think more critically about things, we can make better informed and more ethical decisions.

Education takes time - you can't educate everyone to the same standard overnight - otherwise, we'd all be a modern-day Albert Einstein. But education, time, and open dialogue open the doors to more diversity, inclusivity, improved legislation and cooperation. I have no doubt the world will change beyond recognition, and it's so important that we have that moral compass tucked away in our handbags or in our pockets - so our journey forward can be as smooth as possible.

Maintaining your moral compass means being humble and understanding that you're part of something bigger than just yourself. In the big picture of humanity, our moral values are all connected, and the choices we make affect everyone. If you let go of your moral compass, you not only lose your personal integrity but also lose the connection to the journey we're all on together as human beings.

Remaining calm in the face of adversity is a strength. When the storms of life threaten to pull you off course, the calmness derived from your principles will steady the ship. It is the quiet assurance that no matter the challenges, you will navigate through with integrity, guided by the values that define your moral identity.

But navigating life with a moral compass does not mean standing still. It means being open to change, growth, and the dynamic evolution of understanding. It is a recognition that, just as the stars guide sailors across the ocean, our moral compasses must adapt to the changing skies of experience. Embrace new perspectives, challenge assumptions, and let your moral compass evolve with the wisdom we draw from the journey.

So, as you read these lines, consider the profound implications of not dropping your moral compass. It is not just about personal integrity but about contributing to a world where values are not relics of the past but lights showing us the path forwards. In the ballroom of life, let your moral compass be your dance partner — a steadfast companion that remains true to the tune of your principles in life's trials and tribulations.

In essence, not dropping your moral compass is an act of Getting Over Yourself . It is a recognition that life is not solely about individual pursuits and short-lived pleasures but about our shared responsibility to uplift everyone else around us. When we anchor ourselves in principles that move beyond the temporary, we become architects of a collective legacy of compassion, justice, and authenticity.

Therefore, my friends, let this be an invitation to polish that moral compass with introspection. Let it be the steady rhythm guiding your steps, but let's all throw our arms open to embracing the challenge of staying true to your principles while remaining available to the melodies of change.

Don't Drop Your
Moral Compass

FOOD FOR THOUGHT QUESTIONS ...

1) Reflect on a time when you faced a challenging decision. How did your moral compass guide you, and what impact did it have on the outcome?

2) Are there any historical or fictional figures whose moral compass you admire? What aspects of their values resonate with you, and how can you apply them in your own life?

3) How do you communicate your values to others, and how do you respond when others challenge or question your moral stance?

CONCLUSION
THE END IS NIGH

"YOU DON'T HAVE TO SEE THE WHOLE STAIRCASE TO TAKE THE FIRST STEP"

As we approach the final pages of "Get Over Yourself," let's take a moment to reflect on the journey we've been on together. Throughout these chapters, we've explored the complexities of modern existence, shared laughter, and hopefully filled up on the food for thought banquet. As we stand at the crossroads of conclusion, let's not merely see an end but an opening—a gateway to a refreshed perspective on life.

Throughout this book, I have often questioned why I decided to christen this book 'Get Over Yourself .' It seems patronising, and I didn't want anyone to think I was a self-righteous prick, because I'm not perfect. However, I must say, it's a fitting title—Getting Over Yourself is about becoming less self-centred, increasing our humility, and looking at things with a broader perspective. Most importantly, it means to stop being unhappy about something. I'm not sat here saying that everyone should always be happy; that would be bonkers of me. Everyone will experience the 'down and out' feeling at some point —no one is exempt from life's challenging obstacles.

I mentioned in the first few pages of this book that society seems like a compass gone haywire. I still believe that. But whilst penning this book, it has also given me food for thought—what is the answer? If I did a crash course at Hogwarts and had all the magical abilities that non-muggles have, what spell would I cast to stop that compass from going haywire? The answer is there isn't one. There is no silver bullet to our complicated existence. There are things we're great at, and things we're shit at. There will be areas where we are disciplined and others with no willpower. But I have concluded that we are the solution, just as much as we are the problem.

So, let's reflect. We spoke about enjoying the moment. If we want to embrace and appreciate the present without being overly preoccupied with the past or future, it's ours for the taking. Let's be mindful of the sights, sounds, and sensations around us. Let's brush the distractions and worries aside. Imagine yourself sitting in the park, feeling the sun's warmth on your skin, listening to the leaves rustling, or observing the nature around you. Open your senses to what's in front of you and leave the worries of the past or the thoughts of the future to another time.

Life is a treadmill with no off button, albeit we all run on different speed settings. It can be relentless at times. That's why it's important to shout 'Fuck It,' purposefully tripping yourself up and forcing yourself off that treadmill. It will be there, waiting for you to jump back on after you've had that much-needed burst of spontaneity.

You might disagree, but we've never had it so good. Despite all the bad things happening in the world, there is much to be optimistic about. We need to start looking at the way the glass is filled. Of course, we should be critical of things—pessimism encourages many positive things. But even if the glass may be half empty, it's also half full. Let's reverse the scales of optimism and pessimism and turn that frown upside down.

We must pack for all weather conditions because uncertainty lies ahead, folks. Don't sigh because it's a good thing. We could all do more to leave our comfort zones. But to move forwards, you have to get comfortable with the uncomfortable. We're all creatures of comfort, and there's nothing wrong with that. You'll be a nervous wreck if you live your life constantly outside your comfort zone. But let's cross the border more often and push ourselves to the land where we can face our fears, improve on yesterday, and experience new things.

Remember to dim the lights on your social spotlight. Being social is the key to authentic connections but posting your dinner on Instagram or dancing to the latest trend on TikTok is what I call a 'fonnection.' It's a fake connection. It may seem like people are interested in the dinner you've uploaded and covered in filters but think about whether people genuinely care. Do you get value from them giving you that temporary dopamine hit? We can get so much value out of disconnecting properly!

Get yourself down to the bureau de change—remind yourself to change up some appreciation currency. Let's recalibrate and look at our lives. Our lives are not perfect — perfection is an illusion. But there is so much to appreciate. I challenge you to listen to yourself—the next time you or your inner voice says the word 'hate,' consciously or subconsciously—ask yourself why. Plenty of things get on my tits, and it's good to realise the things that need improvement. But there is so much in life to appreciate that we often overlook.

We're all different—thank God. Imagine if everyone looked, thought, and acted the same—it would be terrible. While everyone being different is one of life's blessings, it also is one of the things that tears us apart. We regularly see football fans scrapping despite their shared love of the game. We see people shouting at each other in Westminster despite us all believing in democracy. Now, I'm not expecting Millwall fans to start going around and hugging everyone—but we can and must be differently united. There is more in this world that unites us than divides us.

To be differently united, you also need to be kind. Let's kill the keyboard warriors with kindness and think about what we can do to be kinder to the people around us, no matter how big or small. Let's bridge the divides and find that collective spirit that reminds people that we've got each other's backs. Ultimately, we're all cut from the same cloth, and you never know - that tiny act of kindness could be just the thing that someone needs.

We love being in control. We often control our emotions, finances and eating habits. Control allows us to embrace the mantra 'everything in moderation', but control is absolutely critical when it comes to comparison. We spend too much time focusing on other people - the clothes they wear, the car they drive, and their lifestyle. You don't need to be looking at other people; you need a mirror, my friend. Gaze into that mirror and self-reflect on what you have and want to achieve for yourself - because we spend too much time impressing other people rather than impressing ourselves.

Then, there is the one thing you should always have in your pocket - your moral compass. The thing that binds all our values and principles together, helps us make decisions, take action and embrace all the trials and tribulations that come our way. If you feel like you need one, create one. If you have one but last used it a while ago - dust it off. And if you have one and use it frequently, don't drop it! Let's be aware of the type of people we are and what we stand for and believe in.

There may have been times throughout this book where

you've thought some of the chapters are similar - you're right. There is a fine line between each chapter - some sharing similar meanings and philosophies. The most important part of this book is the spine - because it brings everything together. All these chapters intertwine like the strands of hair in a French plait. To enjoy the moment, you need to be unsocial. To be differently united, you need to be kind. To be glass half full, you need to not hate but appreciate.

"Get Over Yourself " isn't a manual for radical transformation. It's not a grand revelation promising to unveil the universe's secrets. Instead, it's a collection of reflections—a series of nudges to remind you that, amongst the mountains of self-help advice, there's beauty in the simplicity of just being human.

The chapters we've delved into have hopefully stirred questions within, prompted self-reflection, and nudged you to ponder the intricacies of our shared human experience. "Get Over Yourself " wasn't just a title; it was a call to peel back the layers of introspection, to question whether the world is truly as dire as we sometimes make it out to be. I was totally open to the fact that you may read this book and think it's total bollocks. I really hope you haven't - but if you have, them's the brakes.

So, as we step away from this book and say au revoir, let the echoes of its words accompany you on your onward journey. Let's approach life with curiosity, embrace the moments of beauty, and recognise the shared heartbeat that unites us all.

So, let's raise a glass. May our futures be lived with open hearts, open minds and open eyes. The journey to Getting Over Yourself is never-ending - so keep yourself buckled up because you'll need to ride the rough with the smooth. In the least morbid way possible, we're all on life's journey that eventually leads to the same destination. Some will sadly arrive at that destination sooner than others - but whilst we're here, sharing this journey together, let's make the most of it and make it one to remember.

THANK YOU'S

I COUNT MY BLESSINGS

"IT'S NOT WHERE YOU ARE IN LIFE, IT'S WHO YOU HAVE BY YOUR SIDE THAT MATTERS"

I'm so blessed to live a life bursting at the seams with love from my friends and family. Firstly, I'd like to thank my wonderful and supportive parents and my two amazing brothers. You have always taught me how to Get Over Myself, giving me the best advice, championing me when I'm high and lifting me up when I'm low. I know you don't get to choose your family, but if I had to choose, time and time again, it would be you.

My wonderful extended family. I am privileged to be wedged between so many loving families who have undoubtedly given me a life of fun, love and laughter. Thank you for all the Christmases, birthdays, weddings, baptisms, family meals and gatherings. I hit the jackpot with you folks.

For my friends who have been my biggest cheerleaders, my biggest challengers, and my ride-or-dies. My Aces Brothers, the RGM, Chris, Alex, and Claire - you folks are simply the best.

To a fantastic group of remarkable people who are my sounding boards and continuously give me food for thought through thought-provoking conversations. You folks always gas me up.

Thank you, Herkern, Mehar, Jeevi and Jas, for all your support. Big love to you all!

To Joyce, the lady in the coffee shop who I always enjoy talking to, thank you! You are a true example that kindness still exists in the world.

Finally, a heartfelt thank you to you. Your choice to embrace this book warms my heart. If you've journeyed this far, I sincerely hope it has brought you joy and sparked reflections within. As you close the final pages, consider paying this experience forward by sharing the book with someone dear to you. Let's persist in championing one another, igniting inspiration, and propelling our collective progress. Together, may we rise above our individual selves and truly Get Over Ourselves.

YOUR THOUGHTS ON
GET OVER YOURSELF MATTER!

If you enjoyed Get Over Yourself , help others discover this book by sharing your feedback on amazon. Your review could be the spark that inspires someone to embark on the never-ending journey to get over themselves.

Printed in Great Britain
by Amazon

37687758R00106